A HOTEL ON MARVIN GARDENS

BY NAGLE JACKSON

DRAMATISTS
PLAY SERVICE
INC.

A HOTEL ON MARVIN GARDENS
Copyright © 2000, Nagle Jackson

All Rights Reserved

SPECIAL NOTE

Anyone receiving permission to produce A HOTEL ON MARVIN GARDENS is required to give credit to the Author as sole and exclusive Author of the Play on the title page of all programs distributed in connection with performances of the Play and in all instances in which the title of the Play appears for purposes of advertising, publicizing or otherwise exploiting the Play and/or a production thereof. The name of the Author must appear on a separate line, in which no other name appears, immediately beneath the title and in size of type equal to 50% of the size of the largest, most prominent letter used for the title of the Play. No person, firm or entity may receive credit larger or more prominent than that accorded the Author. The following acknowledgment must appear on the title page in all programs distributed in connection with performances of the Play:

"A Hotel on Marvin Gardens" was originally produced at the
Denver Center Theatre Company
A division of the Denver Center for the Performing Arts
Donovan Marley, Artistic Director
A US WEST World Premiere

SPECIAL NOTE ON SONGS AND RECORDINGS

For performances of copyrighted songs, arrangements or recordings mentioned in this Play, the permission of the copyright owner(s) must be obtained. Other songs, arrangements or recordings may be substituted provided permission from the copyright owner(s) of such songs, arrangements or recordings is obtained; or songs, arrangements or recordings in the public domain may be substituted.

A HOTEL ON MARVIN GARDENS was produced by the Denver Center Theatre Company (Donovan Marley, Artistic Director) in Denver, Colorado, on September 23, 1999. It was directed by Nagle Jackson; the set and costume design were by Michael Ganio; the lighting design was by Don Darnutzer; the sound design was by Matthew C. Swartz; the production manager was Rick Barbour; and the stage manager was Paul Jefferson. The cast was as follows:

KC .... Nance Williamson
BO .... John Hutton
ERNA .... Annette Helde
HENRY .... Sam Gregory
ROSE .... Lauren Berst

The understudies were Morgan Hallet, Matt Pepper and Christen Simon.

CHARACTERS

KC — (pronounced "Casey"). Handsome woman in her 40s.
BO — real name Robert. Late 40s, hale and hearty.
ERNA — attractive in a sort of eccentric way, 40.
HENRY — late 30s, bookish.
ROSE — in her very pretty 20s.

PLACE

One of the Thimble Islands off the coast of Connecticut in Long Island Sound.

TIME

The present.

A HOTEL ON MARVIN GARDENS

ACT ONE

Scene 1

The scene is KC Custer's house on one of the Thimble Islands off the coast of Connecticut. These islands are minuscule, some, like this one, only large enough to contain one house. We are in the main room of the house. It is expensively furnished and loaded with "stuff": objets d'art, gadgets, baskets, dried floral arrangements, stereo equipment, etc. Chic modern paintings on the walls and a picture frame video screen on one. There is a fireplace stage right and down right a door to the bedroom and bathroom. Upstage an alcove and off of it, unseen, the kitchen. The front door is stage left with a clothes closet nearby. There's a big comfy sofa upstage of the fireplace and facing downstage toward it. Just a bit left of center a game table has been placed with four chairs and a Monopoly board in the midst of being set up by: KC, a woman in her forties, very smart and attractive, and she knows it. Bo, A man in his prime, greying, fit and amiable at all times. They are both casually dressed. It's about ten in the morning on April first.

KC. *(Pronounced "Casey.")* ... six twenties ... and two fifties, right? *(They are distributing Monopoly money.)*
BO. Yeah. Think so.

KC. Think so?

BO. Know so.

KC. Seems like a funny number: six twenties.

BO. It all adds up.

KC. Seems funny. *(They continue working silently.)* I hope you're not losing it, Bo.

BO. I'm not losing it.

KC. 'Cause if you're losing it you know …

BO. I know.

KC. History.

BO. Right.

KC. I need a right-hand man I can count on.

BO. I agree.

KC. You agree with everything.

BO. I'm an agreeable guy. *(KC stops her activity for a minute.)*

KC. You know, I did enjoy the French version.

BO. Beg pardon?

KC. Of Monopoly. Last year when we used the French board.

BO. No one could read the cards.

KC. Illiterates. Monolinguals. It was so much fun buying the rue de la Paix and Boulevard Saint Germain. Instead of dreary old Marvin Gardens.

BO. You love Marvin Gardens.

KC. And the Chance cards were funny: "You have been arrested for public drunkenness. Pay five hundred francs." We should get a different language each year. Broaden our horizons. *(She goes back to arranging money, title deeds, etc.)*

BO. Who's Henry bringing?

KC. I always leave that up to him. No one difficult, I hope.

BO. Female?

KC. He always does. But I think Henry's been experiencing a bit of ambiguity in the s-e-x department lately.

BO. What?!

KC. Can't make up his mind. You know, if he's gay or straight.

BO. I didn't think that was the sort of thing one decided.

KC. Oh it's popular right now to, you know, waver.

BO. "Male and female created He them."

KC. But then left no ground rules, except horticultural warnings.

If it weren't for the snake they'd still be in the garden, oohing and
ah-ing over the rhododendron. I've always felt Cain had a mad
crush on Abel … And where did those wives come from? They had
to be their sisters. Our whole race is descended from inbreds.
Which explains a lot, actually … there, the title cards are in order.
(She gets up from table and putters about, arranging furniture, etc.)
They'll be here soon.

BO. Armand left thirty minutes ago.

KC. He's picking up some last-minute stuff for me in Branford.
Then he'll get Henry and whoever at the train station. Whomever.

BO. Is he going to fix the boat? The motor sounded awful coming out here last night.

KC. In fact, he's going to leave us stranded for the day while he
takes it over to the service dock. I told him "fine," because we
won't need anything anyway. He should have it fixed by evening,
and people always stay for dinner, so … *(Getting an ashtray.)* I suppose Henry will smoke.

BO. Nope. He really, finally quit.

KC. I'll believe it when I see it.

BO. 'Strue. He's been doing a lot of odd things lately.

KC. Yes, well … I'm dealing with that.

BO. Beg pardon?

KC. Do you think people still like hard candies?

BO. I hope you're not interfering with Henry.

KC. Do you know that Vic's Variety Store doesn't carry *Me* anymore.

BO. It's just a little convenience —

KC. The only place I can buy *Me* is the train station in New
Haven, and then only at the first of the month.

BO. Subscriptions are … okay.

KC. It was meant for the impulse buyer. That's why I called it *Me*.
It's not the goddamn *New Yorker.*

BO. I don't think anyone's confused about that.

KC. What's that supposed to mean?

BO. Well, the whole format —

KC. You see, Henry thinks it is the *New Yorker*. He's trying to get
all these sensitive poets and fiction writers, or he tries to do a three-
part series on the National Weather Service … I mean, what's that

got to do with the price of bananas? People who buy my magazine are interested in one thing: themselves. *Me* magazine. Self-help, self-promotion and self-gratification. What everyone thinks about ninety percent of the time, but I was the first person to nail it to the wall.

BO. You don't have to pitch it to me, KC, I'm —

KC. "What have you done for *Me* lately?"; that's our motto, Bo. But Henry's getting bored or burnt out or … I don't know what.

BO. He's getting sentimental, that's all.

KC. What?

BO. I found him up on the penthouse roof the other day. "Look at this world, Bo!" That's what he said.

KC. "Look at this world"?

BO. Yep.

KC. What's that mean?

BO. It means … you know, the world.

KC. The world?

BO. Look at it.

KC. I see. Well, I have my plans for Henry.

BO. You're not going to fire him?! *(Pause.)* Oh, KC …

KC. He's been editor-in-chief for ten years. That's enough.

BO. But who —

KC. I have my plans.

BO. You mean you asked him over here, knowing —

KC. It's a tradition. He'd think something was up if I didn't. Every April Fool's day we play Monopoly.

BO. Have you discussed this with the board?

KC. I'll discuss it when it's done. I'm discussing it with my publisher right now, aren't I?

BO. This is going to be terrible. What can we talk about? Oh, KC, I think this is a big mistake. *(She looks at him in amazement.)*

KC. Are you disagreeing with me?

BO. Not exactly … But you'll find that other people —

KC. Would I be living out here on this little island if I cared about other people? Think about it, Bo.

BO. "No man is an — "

KC. But every woman is. If she's got any brains at all. If Daddy taught me nothing else —

BO. Sometimes I think he did.

KC. What?

BO. Teach you nothing else.

KC. God knows he learned the hard way. About not relying on other people.

BO. I know that, KC. And it was terrible what happened to him, but you can't let something that happened years ago —

KC. All I want is to run everything and always be right. Now is that asking so much?

BO. What do you enjoy? I mean really enjoy? Have fun with? Go: "Ha-Ha!"

KC. *(Very seriously.)* I enjoy having sex with you, Bo. Always have. It's something you do really well. And I love sleeping alone when it's over.

BO. I wish you wouldn't always kick me out of the bedroom the minute it's —

KC. I'm not going to discuss it. We've been friends and lovers for many years, Bo. Much longer than any of our married friends. Because we understand the importance of doors.

BO. Ah. Not that I'm disagreeing —

KC. You never outright disagree. But you're sly.

BO. I agree.

KC. *(Suddenly kittenish. Hugs him.)* Of course you do … 'cause you're my great big Bo Brumbley-bundley bear, aren't you!

BO. Well, I …

KC. Yes you are! Say it: You're my great big …

BO. I'm your great big … what was it?

KC. Bo Brumbley …

BO. … bundley … whatever

KC. I hear the launch. *(Bo looks out the big bay window in the "fourth wall" downstage.)*

BO. Yeah. Here they come …

KC. *(Looking out with him.)* Who's the female?

BO. Can't see. She's got that thing over her head. Hood.

KC. We'll do coffee first, then Bloody Marys at eleven —

BO. If everyone drinks.

KC. Oh, I've got some sappy Chardonnay or Perrier water if she's one of those.

BO. This is going to be dreadful.
KC. It's going to be fun. Enjoy the drama.
BO. I hate drama.
KC. Be a dear and give Armand this ... *(She hands him some money.)* ... I owe him for the hot dogs and the beer.
BO. Hot dogs and beer?!
KC. Lunch. We're being all-American.
BO. Thank God. Promise you won't put them in pita bread or something.
KC. Good, they've docked ... Oh my God!
BO. What?
KC. It's Erna Tinker. He's invited Erna Tinker!
BO. Who's she?
KC. Do you ever read the magazine you publish? She's the new restaurant critic. Oh Christ ... hot dogs and beer!
BO. She'll probably love it.
KC. Saucissons de Francfort ... Alsaciens!
BO. What? *(The door-knocker outside raps loudly. KC opens the door, beaming.)*
KC. Hi! Erna! What a treat! Henry, you continually amaze!
ERNA. Hullo, KC! *(Erna is forty, a bit "used," but colorfully attired with all sorts of scarves and bracelets, etc. Right now she is wearing a duffel coat, which she will remove. Henry is perhaps a couple of years younger than the rest of this crowd. He looks ruffled and cleans his glasses a lot.)*
HENRY. You said: "Bring someone interesting."
KC. *(To Erna.)* It's dear of you to come all this way from Manhattan ...
BO. Henry ...
HENRY. Bo. Here. *(He hands a large grocery bag to Bo.)*
BO. I'll just take this into the kitchen ...
KC. *(Still to Erna.)* ... I mean just for, you know, our silly little game and nothing special at all to eat.
ERNA. Oh please, I'm sick of "special."
KC. Well, still ...
ERNA. Last night I went to this horrid German place up on York. Sausages, sausages, sausages. And eight thousand kinds of beer!
KC. Ah ... *(Bo reenters from kitchen.)*

BO. I'll go check with Armand. *(To Erna.)* Hi. I'm Bo.
ERNA. Yes, I know! I'm Erna.
BO. Good! *(He exits.)*
HENRY. *(Going to "window.")* Look at this, look at this!
KC. What?
HENRY. The view! The bay … the little boats … oh God … *(He is crying.)*
KC. Are you all right?
HENRY. Oh yes. Yes! KC, I've found a therapist. At last. After years of denial, telling everyone I'm fine. I've found this wonderful woman who's showing me what a disaster I really am. The scales fell from my eyes. I had never really looked at anything. But now … oh, what is that?
KC. It's a sea gull, Henry.
HENRY. Perfect.
ERNA. *(Who has been wandering around the room.)* Look at all these things! I adore conspicuous consumption. When it's good; I mean you've got everything.
KC. Well …
ERNA. You must be personally responsible for half the GNP. I think it's only too super. And this house … and this island! I mean, your own island!
KC. All these little islands are privately owned.
ERNA. "All these little islands" … it's too dear. But what do you do when you need something? You know, like a sudden pinch of saffron?
KC. Well, the launch —
ERNA. I adore your gondolier.
KC. Armand.
ERNA. "Armand"! So cunning. You and Lady Chatterly, I'll bet: "I'm going to my island with Armand." It's too moist; I love it. Oh! Look at this paperweight. Imagine doing that with, you know, dirt.
HENRY. *(Looking at game setup on table.)* Look: "The table was set by the window with care" … Monopoly.
ERNA. Henry told me you played Monopoly; I adore Monopoly. Haven't played since those rainy days at Schroon Lake when I was a kid.
KC. I'm glad you like it. *(Bo reenters, front door.)*

ERNA. I do. I always win, by the way, so be advised.

BO. Don't count on it. KC always wins, too. We've never really met. I'm Robert Windham.

ERNA. *(As they shake hands.)* The famous Bo. As in "Brummel"?

BO. As in "Bo."

ERNA. Too southern!

BO. Grand Rapids, Michigan, actually.

ERNA. *(Disappointed.)* Oh. Isn't that where they make furniture? *(Henry is still examining the table.)*

HENRY. And the hard candies! You didn't forget … *(He wipes away a tear.)*

KC. Shall we sit? We've got a long day ahead.

ERNA. Oh, can I go wee-wee?

KC. It's right through there.

ERNA. Goody. All that navigation, you know. All that water. *(She exits, doorway D.R.)*

KC. Henry! How dare you bring Erna Tinker without warning me?!

HENRY. What? You said —

KC. Yes, I know "I said," but you always bring someone … uneventful.

BO. It'll be fine.

KC. Now I've got to invent a "lunch." Has Armand left?

BO. Yeah. Boat just pulled away.

KC. Damn.

HENRY. You mean we're marooned? How wonderful!

KC. Armand's got a cellular. I can always phone him.

BO. Let him get the damn launch fixed. That engine'll blow up someday, and then where will you be?

KC. Out of saffron.

BO. What?

HENRY. Who sits where?

KC. You and Erna close to the window so you can look out and register awe.

HENRY. *(Looking out window.)* There are flowers. Crocuses. April is not the cruelest month … "Mixing memory and desire" … I know what that means now. KC, we've got to do a series on the senses.

KC. *(Who has not been paying attention.)* The census?

HENRY. Yes! An issue for each one.

KC. What are you talking about? We're not that kind of magazine.
HENRY. We are. What could be more *Me* than the senses? I smell, I taste, I feel —
KC. Oh, "senses." I thought you meant, you know, the National Census.
HENRY. The National Senses! What a concept! What the nation hears, what it smells —
BO. No, Henry. She means counting.
HENRY. What?
BO. The population. Taking a census.
HENRY. Oh. Oh, with a "c."
BO. Right.
HENRY. Oh. *(Pause.)* Well that could be interesting. "Me and the Census."
KC. Count me out. *(Erna enters.)*
ERNA. Right. I adore your guest towels. Dear little ducks. And I just recalled … *(To Bo.)* … well, as I was sitting there functioning, who you are. You're our publisher.
BO. That's right.
ERNA. Isn't that just too great. Now …
HENRY. *(Holding chair for her.)* You sit here, Erna.
ERNA. Thank you, kind sir. *(They all sit.)*
BO. Splendid. Get ready for a long sit.
ERNA. Right. *(Now Erna begins her rites: She removes a pillow from her gigantic bag and puts it at the small of her back. She takes out a pair of huge spectacles on a gold chain, which she slips over her head and puts on. She removes several gold bracelets and bangles from each wrist. She kicks off her shoes and puts on airline socks. Finally, she dons a green eyeshade, the kind professional card sharks wear. The others all watch silently. Then:)* Let's play Monopoly.
KC. Everyone choose a marker, except —
ERNA. Oh, the top hat! I always love the top hat. Remember top hats? My father —
BO. Er … KC always —
KC. I was going to say, "except the top hat which is always my marker."
ERNA. Oh.
KC. It's a superstition, I know.

HENRY. It's true, Erna; KC always has the top hat …
ERNA. *(Cheerily.)* Well, it's your house. And I love it! *(Looking around the room.)* My God, it must have cost a fortune.
KC. It was my father's.
ERNA. I adore old money … *(Picking up a piece of Monopoly money:)* This money looks old.
HENRY. We've used this same set for ten years. Except for last year …
BO. Oui, oui.
ERNA. *(Misunderstanding.)* What?!
HENRY. KC had this wonderful French version with the Champs Elysees and the Boul Miche. But we couldn't read the Chance cards. Or "ze community caisse" or whatever it was. So we made her get out the old reliable. That was awful of us, KC. I see that now. So limiting.
KC. "Provincial" is the word you're looking for, Henry. But that's history. Choose a marker, please.
ERNA. I'll take this lovely little whatever-it-is.
BO. Hot damn; I get the car!
ERNA. You're so male.
HENRY. I'll just take this.
ERNA. It's beautifully understated, Henry. Too tasteful.
KC. Right then. Now, we've already counted out the money — *(Erna begins carefully counting hers; they watch.)*
ERNA. … eight, nine, ten … right. And one, two, three … right. And six twenties. Isn't that odd? Six twenties. Too odd. And two fifties … Right. *(KC looks at Bo and rolls her eyes in quiet resignation.)* … one, two … and two five-hundreds. I love them. It kills me to break them. All right. Shake for first?
KC. You start.
ERNA. Right. *(She hurls the dice vigorously.)* Two and three is five. Oh dear. That's no good. Henry? *(She passes the dice to Henry, who rolls.)* Ten! Oh, lucky you.
HENRY. KC?
KC. *(Throws dice.)* Three! Good Lord. Bo?
BO. *(Rolls.)* Boxcars! I go first.
ERNA. "Boxcars"! I love that; so professional. Do you go to the casinos?

BO. Naw. I hate playing anything with real money. Except the stock market. So: I go first, and then we go clockwise, Erna, Henry and KC. Right?
KC. Right.
HENRY. Look at that sailboat … waft, waft … *(Bo rolls.)*
BO. Six.
KC. Oriental.
BO. *(Counting spaces.)* One, two, three, four, five, six: Oriental Avenue. I'll buy it.
HENRY. Slum landlord.
BO. *(Correcting him:)* "Emerging neighborhood." I'm banker, by the way.
HENRY. *(To Erna.)* Bo is always banker.
ERNA. Just so long as I'm not.
HENRY. And KC keeps the title deeds.
KC. *(Handing card to Bo.)* Here you are.
ERNA. So many traditions; it's too dear. How long did you say you've been doing this?
HENRY. Ten years. Every April Fools. Ever since I became editor.
KC. It was Bo's idea. The game.
BO. Well, it's a good way to get to know people. Monopoly brings out the worst in everyone. Erna? *(He hands her the dice. Erna rubs the dice violently between her hands. She will always do this, to the increasing annoyance of KC.)*
ERNA. Woodjie, woodjie, woodjie … and go. *(Throws dice.)* Six! And not even doubles. Oh dear.
KC. Oriental.
ERNA. I know.
BO. That'll be six dollars, please.
ERNA. It's too harsh! Here you are, you terrible man.
BO. Thank you.
ERNA. Henry? *(Henry rolls dice quietly.)*
HENRY. Double fives equals ten.
KC. Equals "Just Visiting."
HENRY. "Just Visiting." That's been my life …
KC. Roll the dice, Henry. You had doubles. *(He does.)*
HENRY. Four.
KC. Virginia.

HENRY. Goody. I love Virginia. *(He moves his marker.)* I love the purple color. And it's just on the edge of respectability. My money, sir. *(He gives it to Bo.)*
ERNA. Did you know this entire board is based on Atlantic City?
KC. Yes we did.
ERNA. Oh.
KC. Here's your title, Henry.
HENRY. *(Looking at it.)* "Virginia." Named for the Virgin Queen.
KC. Not much call for that lately. *(She rolls dice.)*
HENRY. Beg pardon?
KC. None of the queens I know are … Three again! Baltic. *(She hands dice to Bo.)*
BO. Aren't you going to buy it?
KC. Baltic? Never. Small potatoes.
BO. Then we have to auction it.
ERNA. I bid thirty dollars.
KC. All right, I'll buy it! Honestly …
BO. *(A la Cagney; to KC.)* Together, sweetheart, you and I are gonna own this slum.
KC. Roll. *(Bo rolls.)* Seven. State.
HENRY. Oh no.
BO. Sorry, Henry. I'm buying into your purple.
HENRY. A day of reckoning will come.
KC. I forgot about coffee. Coffee anyone? It's made.
ERNA. Do you have tea?
KC. *(She hates this.)* Sure.
ERNA. Herbal? *(Pause.)*
KC. I … I should have … *(Getting up.)* I'll look. Coffee, Bo?
BO. Oh yeah.
KC. Henry?
HENRY. No thanks. Winifred says "no stimulants." Until my organs harmonize.
KC. And when they do, may we listen?
HENRY. I know it sounds funny. Bear with me, KC. I need to be borne with.
KC. *(Going into kitchen.)* Two coffees. One herbal tea … *(Exit.)*
ERNA. If you want your organs to harmonize, Henry, you really

should drink chamomile. Too soothing.
HENRY. Good thoughts are best.
ERNA. Good Thoughts? I don't know that brand.
HENRY. No. Good thoughts. Thinking positively.
ERNA. Oh, thoughts.
HENRY. Yes.
ERNA. I see. "There's nothing good nor bad but thinking makes it so." Who said that?
BO. Emily Dickenson?
ERNA. No.
BO. When I hear something pithy I always assume it's Emily.
ERNA. Wasn't she a dear? All alone in that big house. Too haunting. *(KC enters.)*
KC. Would Earl Grey do?
ERNA. Is he decaffeinated?
KC. No, he's just Earl Grey.
ERNA. I'll have a lovely glass of water.
KC. Lovely. Go ahead and play, Erna; it's your turn.
ERNA. Right. Woodjie, woodjie, woodjie … *(KC rolls her eyes and exits.)* Eleven! How exciting. One, two, three, … Ah! Community Chest; goody goody. *(She draws card.)* "You have won second prize in the beauty contest." Oh, KC! I won the beauty contest! I get ten dollars! … *(Disappointed.)* … I must have worn that swimsuit I got at Bonwit's.
BO. Here you are. *(KC reenters with tray of mugs, etc.)*
KC. I think that's perfectly grand, Erna. Here's your water. Bo … Henry …
BO. Where's yours?
KC. *(Snapping.)* I'm getting it! Your turn, Henry.
HENRY. *(Softly.)* I know it's my turn. *(He rolls.)* Five.
KC. *(As she exits.)* New York.
HENRY. … two, three, four, five: New York. I'll buy.
ERNA. Oh yes, those are good, the gold ones.
BO. Two hundred dollars, please.
HENRY. There you are.
BO. A pleasure doing business with you.
HENRY. Deed, please.
BO. KC! *(She reenters with her coffee mug.)*

KC. I'm coming. Henry wants New York, I know. *(She sits.)* God, I don't own a thing. Baltic!
ERNA. This water is perfect.
KC. *(To Henry.)* Here's your deed.
HENRY. Thank you. I am a man of property.
ERNA. Is it Green Springs?
KC. What?
ERNA. The water.
KC. It's from the well.
ERNA. Oh … how authentic!
KC. My turn. *(Rolls dice.)*
BO. Snake eyes.
KC. My God, can't I get out of the slums? Well at least it's a railroad. I'll buy it. I rather like the railroads.
ERNA. You can't build on them.
KC. No, but they're insidious. Little by little they deplete everyone's cash reserves. I enjoy that. Here's your money.
BO. Pleasure doing business with you. *(KC gives him a weary look.)* You roll again.
KC. Yes, I do. *(KC rolls again.)* Six! That's more like it; St. Charles.
ERNA. I wonder why.
KC. What?
ERNA. St. Charles. I mean, if it were in New Orleans or Missouri … but it's not. It's New Jersey.
KC. I'm sure I don't know. I'll buy.
ERNA. Are you a Catholic, Henry?
HENRY. I was.
ERNA. Oh! So was I!
HENRY. Winifred says I might want to return to "the wellspring of my faith."
ERNA. I sometimes go into St. Patrick's and just sit, you know? And smell all that … wax.
HENRY. Yes …
BO. My friends, we have big trouble ahead. In the purples. I own one, Henry owns one, and now KC owns one.
ERNA. Which is why I shall win.
KC. You don't own anything.
ERNA. Of course not. I'm waiting for the high-priced real estate:

Boardwalk, Marvin Gardens.

KC. Marvin Gardens?

ERNA. I always get Marvin Gardens. And I always put a hotel on it. And I always win.

BO. *(Rolling dice.)* Isn't that a coincidence…?

ERNA. Why?

HENRY. KC always gets Marvin Gardens and puts a hotel on it.

BO. Eight.

KC. Kentucky. *(Bo deliberately moves space by space.)*

BO. Whatta ya know? Kentucky. Mine … *(He puts money in bank; KC gives him title card. Erna takes dice.)*

ERNA. *(Singing.)*
"Oh the sun shines bright
On my old Kentucky — "
(She rolls dice.) Woodjie, woodjie, woodjie … Nine! Atlantic! A yellow! Huzzah!! *(She waves money at Bo.)* Take, take, take! *(Bo takes it; she gestures to KC.)* Give, give, give …

KC. *(Giving card to Erna.)* Yes, yes, here.

ERNA. Now we're in business. Henry?

HENRY. *(Rolls dice.)* Six.

KC. B and O Railroad. Damn.

BO. Early days.

HENRY. I'll buy it. *(Transaction is swiftly completed.)*

ERNA. I had lunch at Grand Central yesterday. Divine oysters with a dear little ravigote. On the side. I can't bear people who smother their oysters in lemon and Tabasco. I mean, oysters have a subtle … silver taste, don't they? Saltwater silver. Oh! I like that. Excuse me. *(She takes a notebook from her bag and writes.)*

BO. Always on the job, I see.

ERNA. When one finds a ringing phrase …

KC. Of course, that "saltwater silver" could be mercury poisoning.

ERNA. KC! Not at Grand Central.

KC. I somehow never think of eating at a terminal.

ERNA. Oh, but you should. And in Paris! Gare de Lyon: Le Train Bleu. One of the most beautiful restaurants in Europe.

HENRY. I haven't been to Paris in so long …

BO. The other day I saw a place called The Terminal Diner. I mean, would you go in there? *(KC rolls dice.)*

KC. Eight. New York!
HENRY. Instantly pay me sixteen dollars.
KC. Whose idea was this to play Monopoly?! *(They all laugh.)*
Detestable game. Here's your filthy lucre, Henry.
HENRY. I adore lucre.
BO. My go … *(Rolls dice.)* … three. To Illinois.
KC. Shoot. You've got two reds.
HENRY. Goddamn communist.
ERNA. *(Taking dice.)* My turn. Woodjie, woodjie, woodjie …
Three.
KC. Shit!
ERNA. *(Shocked.)* What?
KC. Marvin Gardens.
ERNA. One, two … Marvin Gardens! O frabjous day, calloo callay!
I've got two yellows! Here, Mister Banker … two yellows! *(Sings:)*
"You'll wonder where the yellow went … "* Remember that?
HENRY. *(Singing.)* "When you brush your teeth with — "* …
with what?
ERNA. "Fixodent."
BO. "Pepsodent."
ERNA. Really?
BO. Definitely.
KC. *(Sullen.)* Here's the deed.
ERNA. I wonder who he was.
KC. Who?
ERNA. Marvin Gardens. *(KC looks at her in disbelief.)*
KC. It's a place. It's gardens. Like the Brooklyn Botanical.
ERNA. Oh … Oh! Of course. Isn't that funny? I've always pictured
this man: Marvin Gardens.
KC. Your turn, Henry.
ERNA. Well anyway, I own it.
KC. Your turn, Henry. *(Henry rolls.)*
HENRY. Five.
KC. Go To Jail.
HENRY. Oh no …
ERNA. Poor Henry; whatever for?
HENRY. Do I get to roll again? See if I get doubles?

* See Special Note on Songs and Recordings on copyright page.

KC. Not till your next turn.

HENRY. Are you sure?

KC. Am I ever wrong?

HENRY. *(Putting marker in Jail.)* No.

ERNA. Poor thing. I'll come visit you.

HENRY. Will you?

ERNA. Yes. I'll bring you a lovely Genoise cake with a file in it: Genoise à la Bastille. Oh! That's divine. Excuse me. *(She gets out notebook, etc.)*

KC. *(Darkly.)* My turn … woodjie, woodjie, woodjie …

BO. KC!

KC. Well it works for her. *(Rolls.)* Eight. Ventnor!

ERNA. Oh no, my yellows …

KC. Ventnor, Ventnor, Ventnor! There goes your monopoly, Erna.

ERNA. Horrors.

KC. I'll buy!

ERNA. Wanna make a deal?

KC. No deals. It's too early. Here's my money … here's my deed … It's twelve o'clock noon: time for Bloody Marys. Now, we've got us a game!

Scene Two

They are drinking Bloody Marys. Henry is not there. The game has progressed as follows: Bo owns: Oriental, State, Illinois, Kentucky, Mediterranean. Erna owns: Atlantic, Marvin Gardens, Short Line RR, Park Place. Henry owns: Virginia, Tennessee, B and O RR, New York. KC owns: Baltic, Reading RR, Indiana, Ventnor, Pennsylvania Ave. The markers are as follows: Bo on Mediterranean, Erna on Park Place, Henry on Kentucky, KC on Go.

ERNA. … and of course when you say "I'm a food critic," people think: "Oh how divine!" But it is really, actually, a difficult and dangerous profession. The hardest thing is anonymity. And you can't go about heavily veiled. I used to wear this great white turban, but they thought I was a Sikh Hindu … or a Hindu Sikh or whatever, and they didn't serve me alcohol. And I couldn't complain and blow my cover … And it kept hitting the waiters … the turban. They're huge. The turbans … Anyway, I was at the Pain d'Or with Sadie — I love to go with Sadie, who's much better at wine than I am — and they brought us this silly little wine from Provence, and it was okay, you know, nothing to write home about, but okay. So I got the check, and this silly little wine cost over a hundred dollars. I said, "Sadie, are you mad?" Then she got upset and said she didn't order that year but a cheaper year, and I said I didn't think they had years in Provence … so anyway, the Maitre d' says, "Is there a problem?" and I said, "Well, that's a lot to ask for a silly little wine from Provence," and he gets furious and tells me it just won some fabulous award and he only had ten bottles and I should thank my lucky stars, and so on. Now Sadie is in tears. I pay the bill. We leave. And as we're crossing Sixty-Third Street, this empty wine bottle comes flying through the air just over our heads. It lands on this dear little Shih-Tzu who's doing his business … I mean, can you imagine? Ours is a dangerous profession.

BO. Did you give them a bad review?

ERNA. I certainly did not. The Caneton aux Olives was superb. I am a professional. But it just goes to show … Can I have some more? It is a perfect Bloody Mary.

BO. *(Taking her glass.)* Happy to.

ERNA. Of course, when I'm working I never drink anything hard. Burns the taste buds. But here …

KC. Yes.

ERNA. *(Looking out window.)* Oh look: There's Henry on the rocks. I believe he's dancing …

KC. Where did Henry and you first meet? I mean, you were writing for —

ERNA. My dear, I was writing for a zillion little newspapers in, you know, Long Island and New Jersey and so on. No, Henry and I met through Winifred.

KC. The therapist?

ERNA. Yes. I was a wreck.

KC. And are your organs harmonized now?

ERNA. Oh yes. My organs; I'm a regular Wurlitzer. *(Bo brings her a drink.)* Thanks, Bo. You are such a nice man.

BO. We strive to please. KC?

KC. No. I wish Henry would come in. I mean a ten-minute break is a ten-minute break. He knows the schedule.

ERNA. *(Looking out window.)* Oh my God!!

KC. What?

ERNA. Henry: He's fallen in!

BO. Where?

ERNA. Into the sea! Into the sea!! HE'S GOING UNDER! *(Bo races to the door, KC following.)*

KC. The damn fool! Why can't he —

ERNA. April Fool! *(Bo and KC stop in their tracks, turn and look at Erna.)* April Fool … *(Pause.)* April Fool.

KC. How very amusing, Erna.

BO. You see, one of KC's little rules is: no April Fools jokes.

ERNA. Ah.

BO. Yes.

ERNA. Perhaps, since you have … since there are so many little rules, … you should post them.

BO. *(To KC.)* She has a point.

KC. Traditions are not posted.

ERNA. Ah … *(Looks out window.)* Oh dear …

KC. Now what?

ERNA. It's Henry … I do believe he's …

BO. Pissing.

ERNA. … whizzing on the rocks …

KC. Damn! We have toilets! *(She goes to door.)* Henry!

ERNA. Don't yell at a urinating man, KC. It can alter their flow forever.

KC. Good!

ERNA. *(Sotto voce, to Bo.)* Is she always testy like this?

BO. No, no. She just … likes order.

ERNA. Oh, well, who doesn't? *(KC is holding door for Henry, who enters.)*

KC. Henry, get in here. We do have neighbors.

HENRY. Sorry. An urge. Winifred says to follow my bliss.

KC. Going Number One on my rocks is not bliss.
ERNA. "Number One"! Too dear. *(Henry and KC return to table.)*
KC. Whose turn is it?
HENRY. And anyway, your neighbors are on other islands.
KC. They can see. They've all got telescopes.
ERNA. We are never alone, Henry. *(To KC:)* What do you do, dear? In an emergency, what do you do? For instance, if I suddenly got appendicitis? *(Pause.)* Yes?
KC. I'm thinking.
BO. She has a phone. And the launch is usually here.
KC. And there's the horn. We all have these electric bullhorns that make an enormous racket. You blow three times, and anyone out in the bay comes to your island. It's a tradition.
ERNA. Isn't that grand! So, sort of … naval.
BO. It's Henry's turn.
HENRY. I wish I were still in jail. You don't have to think.
KC. Henry, you used to be such an aggressive player. You used to get angry.
HENRY. I know. *(To Erna.)* Isn't that awful?
KC. No! You were great. You were a contender.
HENRY. Well … life's too short, KC. Glide with the river.
KC. Roll with the dice. *(He rolls.)*
HENRY. Six and four is —
KC. Pacific! There goes the neighborhood.
HENRY. Eight … nine … ten: Pacific. Your turn.
KC. Don't you want to buy it?
HENRY. What? Oh, Pacific? No. I never cared for the greens.
KC. But I've got Pennsylvania, and Erna's got North Carolina. It'll be a great bargaining chip later on.
HENRY. *(Listlessly.)* Your turn.
BO. You have to buy or not buy; it's the American way.
HENRY. I'll "not buy."
BO. This property is up for auction.
ERNA. I bid two hundred dollars.
KC. Don't be absurd. Four hundred dollars.
BO. Five hundred dollars. *(KC counts her money.)*
KC. Okay … okay. I'm going to mortgage Baltic.
BO. Fat lot of good that'll do you. A big fifty bucks.

KC. Damn … all right. I've got to get a controlling interest somewhere …

ERNA. I'll buy Ventnor from you for three hundred dollars.

KC. In a pig's eye! I wouldn't let go of Ventnor if my life depended on it.

ERNA. It may. Figuratively speaking.

KC. Then you'd have the yellows.

BO. *(To KC.)* What do you care, if you've got the greens? She'll collect from you; then you'll collect from her. *(Henry, during all this, quietly leaves the table and goes to the fireplace area.)*

KC. Statistics show you have a fifteen percent greater chance of landing on the yellows than on the greens.

BO. Statistics?!

KC. There's a book. They did surveys.

BO. That's absurd. That's like saying you've got a better chance of landing on twelve than on fourteen in roulette.

KC. Surveys don't lie.

BO. Surveys do nothing but lie because they depend on human response, which is flabby, and human memory, which is always self-aggrandizing.

ERNA. *(Impressed with Bo.)* Oh my!

BO. *(To Erna.)* Do you remember how many times you landed on the greens the last time you played Monopoly?

ERNA. All I know is I had a hotel on Marvin Gardens. The rest is lost in a deep mist.

BO. Exactly.

KC. There were these monitored games —

BO. Oh please. And probably played by computers —

KC. — I wouldn't know —

BO. — which removes the emotional factor.

KC. Thank God. Are you disagreeing with me, Bo?

BO. My God, I am.

KC. Henry! What the hell are you doing? *(Henry turns violently around.)*

HENRY. I hate this fucking game!

ERNA. My stars!

HENRY. It's mercenary and ugly and … it's just money and sell and buy and make people pay and —

KC. Don't speak disrespectfully of capitalism, Henry.

HENRY. Yes! Look what it's done to Russia!

BO. Russian Monopoly is entirely different. In Russian Monopoly if you land on my property, I kill you. And besides, how about chess?

HENRY. Chess is a thinking man's game.

BO. Yes it is; yes it is. But it's all about killing peasants, taking prisoners … it's barbaric if you think about it: knights whacking bishops …

ERNA. I never could understand chess. Which is sad because it's so pretty.

BO. My bid stands: five-hundred dollars. Going, going —

KC. Wait! I'm on Go. Did I collect two hundred dollars?

BO. No. Not till you pass Go.

KC. Who made that rule?

BO. You wanna look it up?

KC. Yes!

BO. Where's the book? It's not here.

KC. Oh God, it's probably gone … wait a minute. *(She goes to the game box by the fireplace.)* I keep all the game stuff here … *(She pulls out various games.)*

HENRY. "Clue"! I love Clue.

ERNA. Oh so do I! All that mayhem. I love it when I can be Colonel Mustard.

KC. Damn! Look, I'm sure you collect the minute you land on Go. Why wouldn't you? What else are you going to do except pass?

BO. The gentleman who invented this game, in his infinite wisdom, probably knew some situation exactly like this would occur.

KC. I demand my two hundred dollars!

BO. And you'll get it. On your next turn. Now, my bid is five-hundred dollars for Pacific. Going, going — *(Henry bolts to the table, takes two-hundred dollars from the bank and slaps it down on KC's place at the table.)* Henry!

ERNA. Aaaahhh!

KC. Henry! Stop that! *(Pause.)* This is a civilized game.

HENRY. No it's not! We've all been reduced to savages. Greedy, grasping … I'm sick of it! I'm sick of it in this so-called game, and I'm sick of it in our so-called society! *(He goes to the bar and pours*

out a slug of scotch which he downs. Pause.)
ERNA. *(Looking out window.)* All the little boats … .
KC. I'm making lunch.
BO. What about Pacific Avenue?
KC. It's yours. For — … No it's not! I bid seven hundred dollars, goddammit. Give it to me!
BO. You don't have —
KC. *(Wildly turning over title cards.)* Mortgage this … mortgage this … *(Counting money.)* … take this … Seven hundred dollars! Here's the deed. Deal closed, and when I pass Go I'll de-mortgage these and it will all have been a big fat waste of time, and now I'm getting lunch! *(Exit. Pause.)*
ERNA. *(Rising.)* I'll just give KC a hand in the *cuisine.*
BO. Er … I wouldn't do that if I were you.
ERNA. Why ever not?
BO. Stronger beings than you have been known to come flying out of that room, pale remnants of their former selves.
ERNA. Really?
HENRY. It's a rule. No one goes into KC's kitchen except KC.
ERNA. Oh … well … I'll just take in these glasses. Surely she won't mind that. *(Erna picks up drink glasses and goes into kitchen.)*
BO. Too bad. She had so much to live for … *(Sound of a crash from kitchen. Pause. Erna returns, shaken.)*
ERNA. I think … I'll just take a little stroll … on the rocks. *(She exits, front door.)*
BO. Henry … there's something I have to tell you while I've got the chance.
HENRY. Bo, why don't we just talk about something stupid.
BO. Henry … now, you swear you won't tell KC I told you this: She's … leaning towards firing you. *(Pause.)*
HENRY. In favor of whom?
BO. I don't know. Now, it's not … definite. Please don't mention it.
HENRY. Well, well, well … food for thought.
BO. You take this awfully well, Henry. Now, look: I'm dead set against it. But we made a deal, KC and I, when she sold me on the idea of publishing *Me.* I publish. Period. Editorial assignments are hers as president of the corporation. It's her mag.
HENRY. And she always defers to me for departmental decisions.

BO. As well she should. You've been very good at that. I'm not one hundred percent sure about Erna, but —
HENRY. Erna's a bit of a dingbat, but she's all heart and has a terrific palate. And she writes well. Colorfully … So, KC wants me out … interesting. Food for thought.
BO. You said that. *(Pause.)*
HENRY. Should I have bought Pacific Avenue?
BO. I think so, Henry. But I don't know if you're still in the game. *(KC enters.)*
KC. You two, and I, are going to have hot dogs, okay?
BO. Swell!
KC. And I don't want to hear a word about it.
BO. Right.
HENRY. What's Erna having?
KC. I couldn't give her hot dogs after that production number she did about "sausages, sausages, sausages"! So I "created" a little something.
BO. Fine.
KC. Where is she?
HENRY. After whatever outrage you inflicted upon her in the kitchen —
KC. I just looked at her. She dropped the tray.
BO. We know that look. Ordinary mortals quail.
HENRY. It is affectionately referred to — at the office — as the Gorgon Look.
KC. I see.
BO. Erna's on the rocks.
KC. Is the tide coming in? *(She exits, kitchen.)*
BO. The thing is, Henry, I don't think it's anything to do with you. It's KC. She's going through something.
HENRY. She's too young for that.
BO. No, I don't mean "that." Well, maybe "that." I don't know anything about women's bodies. The insides of women's bodies. But she has been very, sort of … searching, lately.
HENRY. Searching?
BO. Looking for why she's here. What she's doing. You know.
HENRY. She's living in Daddy's summer house, and she's doing very well. Got her own magazine and keeping everyone in line.

Like always. Why she doesn't marry you I don't know, but —

BO. I've never asked. I wouldn't dare. She's made that terrifyingly clear. And then …

HENRY. You like your privacy.

BO. Just like you.

HENRY. Not like me. I don't like my privacy. I know that now.

BO. Henry, it's beneath you to have a mid-life crisis. We're smarter than that.

HENRY. We are?

BO. Well, smarter than to let on. People love to see guys like us go through shit.

HENRY. I don't think I'm going through shit.

BO. Good.

HENRY. I think I've been through shit.

BO. Ah.

HENRY. And now it's time to pull the chain. Why is she like this?

BO. Oh, you know: Daddy and so on. He taught her never to depend on anyone.

HENRY. If only her mother had stuck it out. I mean, how old was KC when Mums ran off with that Scientologist?

BO. Eight. Can you imagine?

HENRY. No, I can't imagine. My parents were so boring. Thank God. *(Erna enters, front door.)*

ERNA. "O ye who have your eyeballs vexed and tired, Feast them upon the wideness of the sea." *(Pause.)* Keats.

HENRY. You're so literate, Erna.

ERNA. The good nuns. They crammed civilization and *belles lettres* into our adolescent ears.

BO. When did you get interested in food?

ERNA. *(Sitting on sofa.)* Oh, you know. Europe and so on. I mean, I never ate a bite in my youth. Then I got a Fulbright and found myself in Dijon. *(KC enters with a plate, heading for Erna.)* All that mustard … all that burgundy … my palate awoke. Eureka! I cried — *(KC puts plate down in front of Erna.)* — My God, what's that?!

KC. Well, the rest of us are having hot dogs.

ERNA. What is it?

KC. It's just a little sort of … tartine nicoise. Or maybe Thon

Mayonnaise under a light fondue of cheese … on an English muf-
fin sort of … and some —
ERNA. Tuna melt!
KC. What?
ERNA. It's a Tuna melt. That's what we used to call them. It's a
"grilled cheese over tuna sal on a raft." Tuna melt on toast, right?
KC. Well, it's a bit more … I threw in some capers and some
Tabasco and —
ERNA. Heaven! I love it. My dear, you are an angel. I never get
to eat anything like this. It was the peculiar garnish that threw me.
KC. I'm afraid the top fell off the paprika when —
ERNA. I adore paprika. Too Hungarian. Bless you.
KC. *(Embarrassed by flattery; to kitchen.)* Hot dogs are coming.
Get back to the game … *(Exit.)*
ERNA. Oh dear, do we eat and play?
BO. I'm afraid so. KC keeps a rigid schedule. *(Erna gets up with
plate and heads for game table.)*
ERNA. Very well. When in Rome. On with the game; bring on
the Christians! Now, where were we? I bought Park Place …
BO. Henry landed on Pacific, and all hell broke loose.
ERNA. Oh that's right. Are you still playing, Henry?
HENRY. *(Sitting.)* I am a player.
BO. *(Also sitting.)* Hear, hear! *(KC enters with a plate of hot dogs
and a bottle of white wine. To KC:)* And it's your turn.
KC. Here are the hot dogs. Fix your own. Bo, open the wine.
BO. Yes, madame.
KC. *(Rolls an "eight.")* Vermont. I'll buy it. I'll deduct it from my
two hundred dollars, thank you very much, and I'll de-mortgage
Baltic.
BO. Be my guest. *(He is busy opening wine; KC deals with money,
deed, etc.)*
KC. A pleasure doing business with you.
ERNA. I love to watch old friends …
HENRY. What?
ERNA. Oh, you three; you know, how you do …
KC. Your turn, Bo. I'll pour.
BO. Fine.
HENRY. *(Pointing to window.)* Look at that.

ERNA. What?
HENRY. Those big black clouds …
KC. Oh no, we're not going to have rain …
BO. *(Sings.)* "Though April showers" …
HENRY. The sea's getting very choppy.
BO. *(Rolls dice.)* Six.
KC. Chance.
BO. I know that. *(Moves. Takes card.)* "You have been elected Chairman of the Board. Pay each player fifty dollars."
ERNA. Huzzah, huzzah! KC, this tuna is delicious.
KC. *(Pleased.)* Really? I'm glad.
ERNA. You know, Henry, we should do a whole thing on old-fashioned "comfort foods." Tuna casserole … and that divine thing everyone used to make with green beans and mushroom soup —
KC. — and onion rings, yes!
ERNA. To die!
BO. And chicken croquettes.
ERNA. Chicken croquettes! When was the last time —
HENRY. Waldorf salad.
ERNA. Which you can't even get at the Waldorf.
KC. I don't know …
BO. Your turn, Erna.
KC. *Me* is for the upwardly mobile. I'm not sure they're interested in —
ERNA. I assure you: The upwardly mobile get downwardly hungry. Woodjie, woodjie, woodjie … Snake eyes! Boardwalk! *(She leaps up and begins dancing.)* "On the boardwalk at Atlantic City" … La, la, la, la, la, la!*
BO. You're too young to know that song.
ERNA. My mother always used to sing it when we played Monopoly. *(Sitting.)* My mother, who was the queen of tuna casseroles, the Venus of Velveeta. *(To KC.)* Give me the deed, good woman; here is the last of my lucre, and I don't care. I own Park Place and Boardwalk. I shall destroy you all. I shall now roll again and pass Go. *(As she rolls dice, to KC.)* Was your mother a good cook?

* See Special Note on Songs and Recordings on copyright page.

KC. I have no idea. Here's your deed. Nobody ever lands on Boardwalk.

ERNA. We shall see ... woodjie, woodjie ... nine. Vermont. How tiresome.

BO. Here's your two hundred for passing Go.

KC. Six dollars, please; I own Vermont.

ERNA. Here you are. Earned by the sweat of my brow. You are very quiet, Henry; it's your turn.

HENRY. Yes.

BO. Can we turn on a light? It's getting murky.

ERNA. The participation of Nature.

HENRY. I'm still thinking about "upwardly mobile."

KC. Come on, Henry. Just play the game.

HENRY. Why not? I have been for ten years.

KC. Please don't wax metaphorical, Henry.

ERNA. This wine is delightful. Springy and gay.

BO. Muscadet.

ERNA. I adore Muscadet. It's so straightforward.

HENRY. *(Rolling.)* Eight.

KC. Oh, for Christ's sake ...

HENRY. Six ... seven ... eight: Boardwalk.

ERNA. Pay me fifty dollars instantly.

BO. "Nobody ever lands on Boardwalk."

KC. Shut up. *(There is a huge gust of wind through an open window, knocking over knick-knacks.)*

ERNA. My stars!

KC. Whoops! It's getting wild out there. *(She to window and closes it.)*

BO. I hope Armand's not out in this.

ERNA. Dear Armand.

KC. No, he'll still be at the service dock.

ERNA. It's so dramatic. What do you do, dear? I mean when it really storms?

KC. Daddy built this place like a bunker. And we've got our own generator if the cables break, which they sometimes do.

ERNA. A lone woman against the sea; so turgid.

HENRY. KC can survive anything.

KC. Thank you, Henry.

HENRY. KC is omnipotent.

KC. What's the matter, Henry?

HENRY. Just an observation.

BO. Can I have another hot dog? *(KC passes him the plate.)*

HENRY. But the question lingers: Where does "upwardly mobile" end? When has one reached "up"? And does one collect two hundred dollars and go on? Or two zillion?

KC. It's my turn. *(Rolls.)*

ERNA. I'm sorry you're leaving Vermont; it's been so pleasant visiting.

KC. Eight. St. James. Oh God, I'm broke. I can't buy it.

HENRY. I'll buy it.

KC. Then you'll have a monopoly of the golds.

BO. Do I smell an auction?

ERNA. I bid … five hundred.

BO. Wow.

ERNA. I'm living like there's no tomorrow.

HENRY. Six hundred.

BO. Seven hundred.

HENRY. Eight hundred.

BO. Too rich for my blood. Erna?

ERNA. Pass.

BO. Sold to the gentleman with the hot dog in his mouth for eight hundred simoliens.

KC. Damn.

HENRY. Is that aggressive enough for you, KC?

KC. Your turn, Bo.

HENRY. Is that "upwardly mobile" enough?

BO. Henry …

HENRY. And when one achieve "upness," what does one do, Katherine Custer?

KC. Are you drunk?

HENRY. On a shot of Johnny Walker and a straightforward Muscadet? I don't think so. But answer my question: How far up is "up"? Is "up" sitting on one's own little island? Running one's own little company: Hiring and firing one's own little employees? Is that "up"? And tell me this: How is it up there? How's the view? When the storm clouds roll in, what do you see? Not that you care; you've got your own generator!

KC. That's quite enough, Henry.

ERNA. Henry, dear, Winifred never counsels —

HENRY. Winifred … KC … Erna … all these women giving me advice. Bo, we are surrounded by upwardly mobile women, fanning us ever onwards and upwards. How do we get back down? I ask you: How do we — *(A knock on the front door! Silence. They are dumbfounded. Knocking again; Frantic.)* Well, for Christ's sake, get the door!

KC. Bo? *(Bo goes to the door and opens it. Wind, rain, and Rose burst in. Bo closes door. Rose is a very attractive young woman in her twenties. She wears jeans and a zippered jacket with a "New England Patriots" sports logo on it. The jacket hood covers her head, but she flips it down revealing her wet bangs and short black hair.)* My God!

BO. Are you all right?

ROSE. Yeah … Oh shit, am I glad someone's here … whoo … Hi! How do you do? …

ERNA. Poor thing … did you swim here?

ROSE. No … no.

BO. *(Leading her towards fireplace.)* Come over here and sit down. Are you alone?

ROSE. Yeah.

BO. We should have built a fire.

HENRY. I can do that … *(He goes to fireplace and begins setting wood, etc.)*

KC. *(Going to Rose.)* How on earth did you get here? Are you okay? We can get you some dry things …

ROSE. Oh yeah … yeah, I'm okay. I got rid of the creep.

KC. What creep? Not Armand?!

ROSE. Armand? I don't know anyone named … No, this guy I met at a party last night says: "You wanna ride in my boat?" and I go: "Not now," and he goes: "No, I mean tomorrow," so I'm like: "Okay, I guess so." I mean, you know, why not?. He seems, like, okay. So anyway, he meets me today at Indian Point at the boat place there, and he's got this little, like fishing boat or something, I don't know, and he goes: "Where to?" and I go: "The Thimbles," 'cause I've always wanted to see these little islands up close, ever since I grew up here on the, you know, mainland. So we, like, push

off and putz around the bay, and he goes: "There's a nice little island to have lunch." Well, I don't see any picnic basket, so I'm thinking, "Lunch?" So, anyway, he pulls up to this island, and I go: "Isn't somebody living here?" And he goes: "Naw. Not till summer." So we pulled up in back there and we get out and he's got this dumb paper bag and a bottle of vermouth or some damn thing and that's "lunch," and right away I know I'm in, like, trouble on some goddamn island with a bozo. And we each have a hit of whatever's in the bottle, and suddenly he's all over me, like now I know he just wants to get in my pants or get a Lewinsky, so I give him a swift kick in the ball-bearings, and he's like: "Bitch!." "Goddamn cock-teaser!" … I mean, hey! What'd I do? I got in his fuckin' putt-putt with him and he's blaming me 'cause I don't want to "do it" on the goddamn rocks. So I go: "Keep it in your pants and get me outta here," and he goes, "Fuck you!" and jumps in his glorified dinghy and takes off. He leaves me on this island and it's starting to rain. That's gotta be a criminal offense, right? So I don't know what to do, and I go to that little, like, shack, and there's nobody there but it looks like it's been lived in, you know, so I could, like, survive. You know, like Robinson goddamn Crusoe, but I'm feeling more like Amelia Earhart. Didn't she end up on an island? But then I think I see something move in the house, so I come up here and pound on the door and, like … here I am. And boy, am I glad you're here. *(Pause. They are speechless.)* I'm Rose. Rose Gulick. I live in Branford. *(Pause.)* I'm a teacher. KC. What?!
ROSE. I teach fifth grade at Jefferson. *(Beat.)* Elementary. *(Erna sits. Slow fade to black.)*

ACT TWO

Scene 1

Game status: Bo owns: Oriental, Connecticut, State, Illinois, Kentucky, Pennsylvania RR, Mediterranean. Erna owns: Atlantic, Marvin Gardens, Park Place, Boardwalk, Short Line RR, North Carolina, Electric Co. Henry owns: Virginia, Tennessee, New York, St. James, B and O RR, Water Works. KC owns: Baltic, Indiana, Ventnor, Pennsylvania, Pacific, Vermont, St. Charles, Reading RR. Henry has houses: one each — on St. James, Tennessee and New York. Board positions: Bo is on Connecticut, Erna is on Luxury Tax, Henry is on Indiana, KC is on Virginia. Bo has just completed his turn and bought Connecticut. They are all playing under a kind of undefined pressure. The fun has gone out of it. Rose is nowhere to be seen. Some lights have been turned on as it is dark and stormy outside.

KC. All right … all right. I see it now.

BO. What?

KC. How this goes. How the board divides.

BO. Oh no …

ERNA. It's my turn.

KC. Hold on a damn minute, Erna, okay? *(Erna is mute.)*

HENRY. Is it "dealing" time?

KC. It is dealing time. *(Henry groans.)*

BO. I'll make drinks

KC. No. No drinks. Let's talk, Bo.

BO. You want my red.

KC. Nope. Nope. I'll give you Indiana.

BO. For what?

KC. For the slums.

BO. What?!
KC.   For Connecticut Avenue which you just bought, plus Oriental and Mediterranean.
BO. That gives you that whole side of the board.
KC. It's chicken feed, Bo. It's low-income housing.
BO. Still …
KC. It's the pits, Bo. I'm giving you a monopoly —
BO. I'm giving you two.
KC. — in the high-rent district. You put a hotel on those reds, you can wipe us out. I put a flop-house on these lots, who cares? It's just an annoyance.
BO. So why do you want them?
KC. That's my business.
HENRY. Just do it, Bo. It'll speed up the game.
BO. You've got a point. *(Pause.)* It's a deal. *(Bo and KC trade title cards.)*
KC. You won't regret it.
BO. Yeah, right.
ERNA. May I please have my turn now?
KC. Hold on just a minute.
ERNA. I thought you could only make deals when it's your turn.
KC. Well, it's your turn, and I want you to make a deal.
ERNA. I'm happy just as I am.
KC. No, you're not, Erna. Look at you: "Poor little rich girl." You've got Park Place and Boardwalk and that's it. I hold the key to your happiness.
ERNA. I assume you refer to Ventnor Avenue?
KC. No …
ERNA. I might discuss the Water Works with Henry.
HENRY. Water Works?
ERNA. I've got the Electric Company.
KC. "Water Works"! "Electric Company"! Utilities? I'm talking land, Erna. I'm talking development property here. I've got an offer that will change your life! *(Pause.)*
ERNA. What is it?
KC. I'll give you … give you: Pennsylvania and Pacific Avenues.
ERNA. *(Lips trembling.)* Then … then I'd have the greens.
KC. You'd have the greens. You'd have all the greens and both the

blues. You'd have the high-rent district. From Pacific to Boardwalk; yours.

ERNA. My stars …

BO. That gives her one-quarter of the board and half the property values!

KC. Right!

ERNA. And … and what do you get? *(Pause.)*

HENRY. Your firstborn child.

KC. I get Atlantic … and Marvin Gardens.

ERNA. Marvin Gardens?! Oh no; I love my Marvin Gardens …

KC. Let it go, Erna. Let this silly obsession, this childhood attachment —

ERNA. I always won with Marvin Gardens at Schroon Lake.

KC. That was Schroon Lake, Erna; this is Long Island Sound. Let it go. Move on.

ERNA. Well …

HENRY. It's a good deal, Erna. You'll wipe us out over there. The only thing you don't own there is the Pennsy Railroad —

BO. — which is mine. Whoopee.

HENRY. Go for it, Erna.

ERNA *(To Henry.)* Why do you want me to? You're losing.

HENRY. Hey! I've got houses. … But you're right, actually. And a man should know when he's through.

ERNA. That's so touching, Henry. Too real.

KC. Cut the dramatics, Erna. Let's get down. It's you and me. The boys are out of it.

BO. "Boys"?

KC. I've got the Bowery, and you've got Sutton Place.

BO. I thought you said I'd wipe everyone out with my reds.

KC. And you fell for it. That's history. Now, whatta ya say, Erna?

ERNA. Marvin Gardens …

KC. It's gardens, Erna. It's just a corner of the board. You've got all the advantages.

ERNA. Get me a drink, Bo. *(Bo, who has been dying to get to the bar, leaps up.)*

BO. Right.

ERNA. Scotch.

BO. Sure thing.

HENRY. Erna …

ERNA. *(Standing.)* I'll do it!

HENRY. Thank God.

BO. Here's your drink.

ERNA. Thanks. *(She downs it in one gulp.)* I hated that.

BO. The deal?

ERNA. The scotch.

KC. *(Handing over title cards.)* Your deeds, madam. And?

ERNA. *(Handing over yellows.)* Good bye, Marvin …

KC. Let's play Monopoly; your turn, Ern. Make with the "woodjie." *(Rose enters from the bath/bedroom area. She is in a white terrycloth robe and has just taken a hot bath.)*

ROSE. What a neat bathroom! You've got covers of *Me* magazine all over the walls; that's so cute.

KC. Yes, well, it's my magazine.

ROSE. Really? Mine is *People.* I even subscribe to *People.*

BO. *(Kindly.)* No, she means it's her magazine; she owns it. And Henry, here, is editor —

ERNA. *(Has rolled dice.)* One, two, three, four, five …

ROSE. Oh, that explains it.

ERNA. Baltic.

KC. I own it. I own both. Pay me … eight big dollars. *(Erna pays her.)*

ERNA. *(To Bo.)* Two hundred for passing Go.

BO. *(Paying her.)* Here.

ERNA. *(Tossing dice to Henry.)* Here. *(Rose is walking around the room, examining things; Henry watches her.)*

ROSE. All this stuff …

KC. What?

ROSE. You've got all this stuff.

KC. Did that nice hot bath take the chill off?

ROSE. Oh yeah, it was neat. *(Pause.)*

KC. Henry?

HENRY. In Bali there are two worlds: *sekala* and *nisekala. (KC rolls her eyes.)*

ERNA. *(Interested.)* Really.

HENRY. *Sekala* is that which can be seen: trees, food … so on. *Nisekala* is that which cannot be seen: the spirits, the gods. These two worlds co-exist. Actively.

ROSE. My God … a TV hanging on the wall like a picture! …

HENRY. The *sekala* and *nisekala.*

ROSE. Does it work? *(No one pays any attention to Rose.)*

BO. *Nisekala?*

HENRY. Yes. An equal reality which cannot be seen.

BO. Because it doesn't exist.

HENRY. What?

BO. It doesn't, Henry.

KC. Could we play the game?

BO. I mean, I'm sure Bali is great, and I love that eye makeup and that finger stuff they do when they dance, but *sekala* and whatever —

HENRY. *Nisekala.*

BO. — is bullshit. Magic, religion, all that. It's like professional wrestling. Keeps the unwashed happy, but even they know it's bullshit.

HENRY. You are comparing the spiritual dimension of man to big-time wrestling?

BO. There is no spiritual dimension, Henry. Everyone knows that. They won't say it. But they know it.

ERNA. You're so bleak.

BO. Look: Can you imagine what would happen if we had hungry lions in the Coliseum today? How many "believers" you know would go play with the cats rather than renounce their religion? Can you see Pat Robertson or the Pope going off to be lunch? I don't think so. They'd cut a deal. They'd sign with the Emperor in a Roman minute.

KC. Will someone please tell me what brought all this on?

ROSE. I agree.

BO. What?

ROSE. *(To Bo.)* I agree with you completely. It's, like, everyone goes to church but no one, like, … really believes all that. But it's nice. The music and all.

HENRY. I'm not talking about religion per se —

KC. I hate "per se"; I thought we were done with "per se."

BO. What you see is what you get, Henry. What do you think, Erna?

ERNA. *(Who is feeling that scotch.)* Well, of course, with me it's all senses, senses, senses. Taking them to a higher plane. One can survive on rice. One can survive on beans. But we can also combine rice and beans at which point Culture begins. Add some herbs and spice, a crayfish or two … Combinations. Putting things together. Yin and yang. Male and female. I'm all for the senses and putting things together. Dialectic. Hegel … Coitus.

KC. Coitus?

ERNA. Oh yes, dear, don't you think?

BO. Erna … you are really something!

KC. Henry, will you roll the dice?

ROSE. I love Monopoly! Can I play?

KC. No. You have to be in at the beginning.

ROSE. *(Looking at her surroundings.)* I guess so …

HENRY. *(Has rolled.)* Five.

KC. Water Works! I can't believe it; the one space he owns.

ERNA. *(To Bo, advisedly.)* The good spirits are guiding him.

HENRY. *Nisekala. (Outside, a huge clap of thunder. The lights flicker.)*

ERNA. There, you see?

BO. You got gas in the generator, KC?

KC. Full up.

ROSE. Whoo! What do you do when the weather gets bad out here?

KC. You deal with it.

ROSE. I bet it's really romantic.

BO. It's whipping up out there …

ERNA. Oh, I hope that dear little … Armand isn't fighting the waves.

KC. No, he won't have left the mainland yet.

ROSE. Jeez. How'm I gonna get back?

HENRY. Don't you worry; you'll go back with the rest of us after dinner.

KC. Of course, maybe I could call Armand. I mean he could come earlier for you.

ROSE. No prob. I'm happy.

KC. Oh. Well … good …

ROSE. I don't have to be anywhere till school tomorrow so, hey — afternoon, evening; I could care less. *(Pause. Bo closes his eyes; he*

knows what's coming.)
KC. *(Calm, deliberate.)* You mean, of course, you couldn't care less.
ROSE. Whatever.
KC. You see, if you could care less, then you do care. You are capable of caring less. Because you care.
ROSE. Well, yeah. But I mean, you know what I mean.
KC. No, I do not. Not if you say the exact opposite of what you truly mean.
ROSE. Well, it's just an expression. Everyone says it.
KC. No, everyone does not say it. You mean you could not care less, and yet you say the opposite … and you expect us to derive the meaning.
ROSE. No one's ever had any trouble before when I —
KC. Because you have been speaking with people who, like yourself, have lost all connection between language and meaning.
BO. KC …
KC. You, who are a teacher in the public schools, have not a clue as to the meaning of words, to the logical structure of words nor, I daresay, to the possible beauty of words.
ROSE. *(To others.)* What'd I say?!
KC. And when we lose the meaning of words we also lose clarity of thought. It appalls me to think of your teaching the young. And my taxes pay for it. *(Pause.)* What do they pay you?
BO. KC!
KC. I'm interested.
ROSE. Twenty-nine. *(Pause.)*
HENRY. What?
ROSE. Twenty-nine thousand.
HENRY. A year?!
ROSE. Uh-huh … Is that too much?
ERNA. My God, I spend that on lunch … Well … I have to …
HENRY. That is deplorable.
ROSE. I work summers at The Seagull. *(Sound: violent thunder.)* Jeez louise.
HENRY. You see, KC? There's your problem. We're spending fortunes on … on advertising … on … on TV programs: ten million an episode for some of that garbage we watch … and sports arenas, and … we've got a class struggle going on here!

KC. Well, it's not my fault.

HENRY. Yes it is.

KC. How?

HENRY. We put out this stupid magazine about getting and having; we ought to call it GIMME!

KC. And we pay a lot of taxes for the privilege. But if standards are not kept —

HENRY. Who sets them?

KC. We do.

HENRY. Who's "we"?

KC. The ... the people who run things.

HENRY. Oh Jesus.

BO. Whose turn is it?

ERNA. KC's.

KC. Good! Thank you. Now: I'm mortgaging all my properties except the yellows. Add that up, Bo, and then take this ... *(Gives Bo a wad of "cash.")* ... and see how many houses I can put up on my properties.

HENRY. You're just closing down this whole side of the board? Mediterranean to Connecticut?

KC. It's just low-income, Henry. Better dump it and build where I can make something.

HENRY. *(Standing.)* Jesus!

KC. Now what's wrong?

HENRY. The symbolism is staggering.

KC. What?

HENRY. What you're doing. Plow down the low-rent buildings. Build these big developments ... Where do you live, Rose?

ROSE. I got a townhouse in Guilford. It's neat.

HENRY. *(Disappointed.)* Oh. Well that's good.

ROSE. But I rent. And I'm afraid it's gonna go, like, you know, condo, and I can't afford that, so —

HENRY. You see? You see, Bo?

ROSE. Look, I'm sorry if I make all this trouble. I'll just sit here and read while my clothes dry.

BO. Here are your houses, KC. Roll the dice, please. *(Thunder. Lights go out.)* And that's all she wrote.

ROSE. Can we light candles? I love candles.

ERNA. Oh, so do I!

KC. I've got oil lamps all around.

BO. *(Rising.)* I'll light them.

KC. Thanks, Bo. And bring one here to the table. *(Bo goes around the room, lighting oil lamps. Brings one to table.)*

ROSE. Jeez, I wonder if they're out in Branford, too. My folks are having a pinochle party.

ERNA. Pinochle! Oh! My father used to play pinochle on Schroon Lake. Those lovely summers … *(Sings, Neil Diamond:)* "I am, I cried"* …

KC. *(Sotto voce to Bo.)* I think we'd better cut Erna off in the d-r-i-n-k department.

ERNA. *(Singing.)*
"Walk right in
Set right down,
Baby let your mind roll on … "*

ROSE. I love those old songs.

ERNA. "Old"? *(Henry goes over to Rose.)*

HENRY. Tell me about teaching.

ROSE. It sucks.

KC. Bo, I think you'd better go out to the pump house —

ERNA. Oooh, the pump house!

KC. — and start the generator.

ERNA. Oh, but the candle light … or oil light … it's so romantic.

KC. Yes, but without the generator the pump doesn't work, and if the pump doesn't work you won't be able to flush when you use the john, and I won't be able to make dinner. Which reminds me, I've got to get some things started.

ERNA. Dinner? You are a saint.

BO. *(Putting on a slicker.)* I'll take a look-see if the other islands are out too.

KC. I'm sure they are. *(Erna runs to the coat closet.)*

ERNA. Oh … oh! Can I go? I'd love to see the storm and feel its wrath. Not to mention the pump house.

BO. Ah … well, here; take this hat. It's better than your hood.

ERNA. Oh! Like a lobsterman. How dear!

KC. *(To Bo.)* Remember the little toggle thing goes to the red mark.

* See Special Note on Songs and Recordings on copyright page.

BO. Right.

KC. And the big black thing pulls out till the engine starts.

BO. I know, I know.

KC. And don't hurt your back pulling on the thing.

BO. I won't.

ERNA. *(To Bo.)* Oh dear, you've got a back? I've got a back, too. *(They exit, front door.)*

KC. So. Rose, do you need anything?

ROSE. Can I have a drink?

KC. Oh my God, I'm sorry. Of course you can have a drink. How rude of us. Henry, get this poor girl a drink.

HENRY. Scotch? Sherry?

ROSE. You got vodka?

HENRY. Sure.

ROSE. And some, like, cranberry juice or o.j.?

KC. In the fridge. *(Rose starts towards kitchen. KC cuts her off.)* I'll get it. *(Exit, kitchen, taking an oil lamp with her.)*

HENRY. KC is very protective of her kitchen.

ROSE. She's lucky. My kitchen? It's right out there in front of God and everyone.

HENRY. Ah.

ROSE. Yeah. It's a drag. *(KC reenters with a little can of cranberry juice.)*

KC. There you are, Henry. So. The lights should come on anytime now. I'm going to get the dinner things started. Is there anything you don't eat, Rose?

ROSE. Squid. I don't eat squid.

KC. Not on the menu. Not to worry. *(Exit.)*

HENRY. *(Mixing drink.)* I can't believe what that sonofabitch did to you.

ROSE. He didn't do anything to me. I gave him a good chop to the meat department. His nuts are gonna look like basketballs.

HENRY. Here's your drink. A Cape Cod, I think they call it.

ROSE. But he deserved it. Still, guys are always doing stuff like that. Guys are interested in one thing.

HENRY. Yes, well, not all guys.

ROSE. Oh, not you guys. *(She drinks.)* Oooh, that's good. Not you, you know, high-class guys. But the nerd-os I get to meet.

Dickheads. Really.

HENRY. You shouldn't think of us as "high-class."

ROSE. Are you kidding? Look at all this. And you talk about really neat stuff. And you play games, and the TV isn't even *on*. I mean, you know, that's class.

HENRY. We're worthless.

ROSE. What?!

HENRY. Really. We put out a trashy magazine that looks like it's "sophisticated." We make too much money or we inherited too much money … We do nothing in this world.

ROSE. Why should you?

HENRY. Because … because one should. You're worth ten of us. Teaching the young.

ROSE. I said I'm a teacher; that doesn't necessarily mean I'm teaching anyone.

HENRY. What?

ROSE. You can't. You can't get through to them. Or there's not enough time, or the kids don't really care. You go through the motions.

HENRY. But you're trying to —

ROSE. Like there's this Mildred Tannenbacher? I love her. And with a name like Mildred she's gotta have a rough time, I mean what were her parents thinking? But of course she doesn't have parents or only one. Lives with her mom who works at Denny's all kinds of shifts. Anyway, I love Mildred and Mildred's hot at math. So am I. I'm a whiz at algebra. But the kids all make fun of her 'cause she dresses dumb and she's got like this speech problem. Says her 's's funny. "Lateral lisp," says the speech therapist — who's a real asshole. But, you know, Mildred's gonna be a systems ana-lyzer or a chemical engineer or whatever if she can survive all these bozos making her miserable six hours a day at school. And when she goes home her mom's too tired to be, you know, a friend. And she doesn't have any friends. Mildred, I mean. At least I get them pre-pubescent. God help us when they get pubes. All they wanna do is go to the mall or grope each other in cars. And they give 'em cars! Their dopey parents. And then there's drugs. And then some dick-on-legs knocks up some lovely girl like Mildred who wants to show she's "one of the gang," and so she ends up workin' at

Denny's … and there's not a thing me or anyone else can do to, like, change it.

HENRY. But you survived.

ROSE. Survived? I'm living on the poverty line with dorks trying to get in my pants and surrounded by idiots. You ever been in a teacher's lounge?

HENRY. No.

ROSE. You wanna see random. You wanna see mediocre! No-brainers arguing over doughnuts and who's making the coffee this week. Helen Beezer complaining about her "menstrual problem," which she seems to have twenty-six days of the month and the other four she's horny. Mr. Harrington — he's the vice-principal — throwing his weight around, which is hard for a guy who weighs, like ninety-eight pounds on a high-pressure day … And then I come here. I see you guys. All this stuff. What life could be …

HENRY. It's empty, Rose.

ROSE. Yeah, but it's empty with style. You ever been to Branford?

HENRY. I want to get out of all this "style."

ROSE. You crazy?

HENRY. My life is like that board game. Only not as interesting.

ROSE. Come on, I'll bet you know, like … Rosie O'Donnell.

HENRY. No I don't. I mean, we've met. We go to a lot of the same functions, but I certainly don't —

ROSE. Jeez, I'll bet you know Donald Trump and Liz Smith and —

HENRY. We have nodding acquaintance, yes, but —

ROSE. Jeez louise.

HENRY. — but they're just "people," you know? And they're not doing anything, either. Putting up buildings. Dishing dirt. Jockeying for position.

ROSE. Well, what do you want to do, Henry? Can I call you Henry? You're, what, the editor, did I hear someone say?

HENRY. Yes.

ROSE. Holy shit. *(KC enters.)*

KC. Why on earth haven't the lights come on?

HENRY. You want me to go check?

KC. No … I'll give them five more minutes … Heavens!

ROSE. What?

KC. You're quite beautiful, aren't you?
ROSE. Me? I look like … I don't know what.
KC. Watch out for Henry; he's in therapy. *(Exit.)*
ROSE. You are?
HENRY. She's going to fire me.
ROSE. Huh?
HENRY. KC. She's going to fire me. She doesn't know I know.
ROSE. What will you do?
HENRY. I don't know. I don't care. I'm delighted, actually. A new life.
ROSE. Lucky.
HENRY. Anyone can have a new life, Rose. Don't you know that?
ROSE. Hey, I owe three thousand on my Visa, I'm paying off a used Honda, and my folks need a check each month since Dad got laid off when the plant he worked at "downsized." *(She makes quotation marks with her fingers.)*
HENRY. *(Impulsively.)* I'll help you, Rose.
ROSE. Hey. I'm no charity case.
HENRY. No, no. I'll … I don't know what. Let's go somewhere.
ROSE. Where?
HENRY. Together. We'll live simply and start anew.
ROSE. "Simply"? You don't even know me, Henry. And I sure as hell don't know you.
HENRY. That's what makes it so exciting. *(Pause.)*
ROSE. You really got a lot of money? Like a million?
HENRY. No, no.
ROSE. Oh.
HENRY. Maybe half a million.
ROSE. Henry! *(Electric lights come on.)*
HENRY. "And there was light." We could start a school somewhere, you and I. Really teach. Save the Mildreds.
ROSE. Yeah, but I wanna meet Rosie O'Donnell and … and Whoopi Goldberg — do you know Whoopi Goldberg?
HENRY. She wrote a piece for us, actually.
ROSE. I don't want to go off to the Adirondacks or … I don't know, Idaho or somewhere and teach. I want … I want this.
HENRY. Oh, Rose. This is boring.
ROSE. Not to me it isn't. This is … this is the dream! *(Erna and*

Bo enter, front door.)
ERNA. It is fantastic out there; so basic!
BO. Where's KC?
ROSE. She's in the — *(KC enters.)*
KC. What took you so long?
BO. The … "thing" was jammed.
KC. The red thing?
BO. No. The other thing.
KC. The pull thing.
BO. Yeah. Anyone want a drink?
HENRY. Yes. Oh yes, goddammit, yes!
KC. Henry … Rose, I'm sure your clothes must be dry by now.
ROSE. Right. 'Scuse me, I'll go change.
BO. Must you?
KC. Bo.
BO. She looks great like that. Doesn't she, Henry?
HENRY. Yes she does.
KC. Well, I'm sure it's entirely up to you. I'm cutting up an egg-
plant. *(Exit.)*
ERNA. It's early for eggplant …
ROSE. I'm gonna change. *(Exit, bedroom area. Henry goes to bar
where Bo has fixed them both whiskeys.)*
HENRY. How will you know if the power comes back on? I mean
the real power.
BO. It's got a dealie … an override. It'll turn off the generator.
(Lightning flash.)
HENRY. Lightning … I'm going out.
ERNA. Wear something rubber, Henry.
HENRY. I won't be long. *(Exit, front door.)*
ERNA. So troubled. They're all so troubled, Bo.
BO. I know. Here. *(Gives her a scotch.)* That was lovely.
ERNA. Yes?
BO. In the pump house.
ERNA. *(Beaming.)* Did you like it? I'm so glad.
BO. It was … fantastic.
ERNA. A little something the boys taught me at Schroon Lake.
BO. I wish I'd been at Schroon Lake.
ERNA. Yes … it's all been downhill since Schroon. Oh, Bo … I

feel suddenly triste.
BO. Don't, Erna.
ERNA. I've made a fool of myself.
BO. No. No.
ERNA. Promise you won't think less of me?
BO. Less of you? I had you pegged for … I don't know … just another foodie. But you … you are a deep, vibrant woman, Erna.
ERNA. "I eat the air, promise crammed. You cannot feed capons so."
BO. What?
ERNA. *Hamlet.*
BO. Ah. You are a woman of … dimension, Erna.
ERNA. Really? Which?
BO. I've been frittering my time.
ERNA. You're a great success!
BO. My daddy made a little money in Grand Rapids … my daddy made a lot of money in Grand Rapids, and I came here to spend it. Only everything I spend it on makes even more. It's the damnedest thing.
ERNA. *(Kissing his brow.)* Good things for good people.
BO. I'm not even remotely good.
ERNA. Really? Good. People who think they're good are inevitably dishonest. Is KC good?
BO. Heavens no.
ERNA. How long have you — ?
BO. A few years. I came out here to talk business once and … well, in fact, the power went out then, too.
ERNA. Not the pump house!
BO. No, no. Armand was here. He did all that. But … one thing led to the next. And then I began to stay over weekends, and stuff accumulated.
ERNA. We are ruled by "stuff." You mean material stuff?
BO. Yeah. Clothes … toilet kit … bathrobe. My galoshes. Stuff.
ERNA. "We are such stuff as dreams are made on/And our little life is rounded — "
BO and ERNA. — "with a sleep" *(They kiss as KC enters.)*
KC. Oh for Christ's sake.
BO. I'm sorry, KC.

KC. My God, a little weather and everyone goes nuts.

ERNA. Yes … *The Tempest* brought us together.

KC. The old pump-house ploy, eh Bo?

ERNA. What?!

KC. Everyone gets into trouble in the pump house. When I was eight, my cousin Ziggy showed me what was what, but I decided I didn't care. Armand regularly boffs the local natives there. It must be something about damp wood and electrical power.

BO. KC, you know I have never —

KC. No, he never has, Erna. Till now?

BO. Let's just say: We had a moment.

KC. Okay, let's just say that. All together now: "We had a — " … Well, come on, come on. *(Bo takes a cellular phone from his jacket pocket.)*

BO. I'm calling Armand. I don't think anyone wants to finish the game.

KC. Oh no you don't! You know how superstitious I am, Bo. We always play Monopoly on April Fools, and I always win. If we don't, and I don't, God knows what may happen.

ERNA. Well, I hate to say it, KC, but all signs point toward my winning this time. *(Bo quietly punches in a number on his phone.)*

KC. You're good, Erna. I've got to hand it to you. You're good. But you're not that good.

BO. *(On phone.)* Armand? Bo … oh really? … Oh dear … well, okay. But when you can, okay? … We're … we're finishing up a little sooner than — *(KC yanks the phone out of his hand.)*

KC. Come as planned, Armand. We're having dinner at seven, and they'll leave after that. All of them … The what was broken? … Well, I don't know what that is, but fix it … *(She clicks off. Hands phone back to Bo.)* Where's Henry?

ERNA. Out.

KC. Out? In that?

ERNA. He's being elemental, I expect. Our therapist is very into the elements.

KC. But it's pouring out there! *(Door opens. Henry comes in. He is only slightly damp.)* Why aren't you soaking?

HENRY. I was in the pump house.

KC. By yourself?! That's disgusting.

HENRY. What?

KC. I am about to serve tea, and we shall resume the game.

HENRY. Oh God …

KC. Henry! Don't be such a baby. *(Rose enters, dressed as when she first appeared, in jeans and a sweatshirt.)*

ROSE. Hi. *(Henry goes to her.)*

HENRY. All dry?

ROSE. Yeah. You're wet.

HENRY. Just a little. *(He takes her hands.)*

KC. Oh for God's sake … I'll get tea. *(Exit, kitchen.)*

BO. We've got to get out of here.

HENRY. I know.

ERNA. How? We're terribly interesting, but I don't think we can walk on water.

HENRY. Still, if it were an emergency …

BO. Armand's got engine problems. He won't be coming till eight or so.

HENRY. Shit. *(KC charges into room holding a kitchen knife.)*

KC. No one's leaving; don't even think about it. Now sit down in your places. Rose, you sit on the couch. We shall have tea and play Monopoly until six. Then we'll have cocktails, and then we'll have dinner. Is that quite clear? *(Lights go out.)* What on earth?! … Henry! *(Henry sits guiltily.)* What did you do in the pump house?!

Scene Two

(One hour later.) Game situation: The entire board has now been bought. Bo owns: the reds, State, Pennsylvania RR. Erna owns: the greens, the blues, Short Line and Electric. Henry owns: the golds, Virginia, B and O, Water Works. KC owns: From Mediterranean through Connecticut, the yellows, St. Charles and Reading RR. Henry has one house on each gold. Bo has three houses on each red. Erna has two houses on each green and blue. KC has four houses on each yellow. Positions: Bo is on Reading RR. Erna is on Free Parking. Henry is on St.

ERNA. … five-six-seven-eight: Free Parking. Goody. We like Free Parking. Henry? *(Henry sighs.)*

KC. Your turn, Henry.

HENRY. This is so pointless.

KC. Almost as pointless as putting water in the generator gas tank.

HENRY. I said I'm sorry.

KC. If you were unhappy here all you had to do was —

HENRY. It is glaringly obvious that I'm unhappy. It is glaringly obvious that we all are.

BO. Not Rose. She's happy.

KC. All you had to do was ask if you wanted to leave the game.

HENRY. You know that's not true. It's play or die around here.

KC. Well, all I can say is, it's lucky I've got a gas stove. The moussaka will be ready on time.

ERNA. Moussaka? You shouldn't have.

KC. You're right, but we're going to have it anyway. Roll the dice, Henry. *(He does.)*

HENRY. Doubles. Eight.

KC. Illinois.

HENRY. Will you please let people count it out?! Why do you insist on announcing each move the minute —

KC. It's a reflex. I know the board by heart.

HENRY. It takes away all suspense.

KC. I hate suspense.

BO. Let's see … with three houses, that's seven hundred and fifty dollars, please.

HENRY. Oh my God. Let's see if I've got … Hey, does anyone want to buy Virginia?

BO, ERNA and KC. No.

HENRY. That's the only monopoly left. Well … I've got to mortgage it. And here's the rest. *(Turns over title card; hands cash to Bo.)*

ERNA. You've got so much money, Bo.

BO. That's my game plan.

KC. It never works.
BO. Time will tell.
KC. Roll again, Henry. You had doubles. *(He does.)*
HENRY. Three. *(KC is silent.)* Well?
KC. My lips are sealed.
HENRY. One-two-three: Ventnor. With four houses. I'm out.
KC. *(Smiling maliciously.)* It's only nine hundred and seventy-five dollars.
HENRY. I'm out.
ERNA. Dear Henry. But you've got those little houses.
HENRY. I've got three houses, Erna. And three properties. Virginia's mortgaged. And I've got the B and O Railroad —
KC. Such an unattractive name.
HENRY. — and the bloody Water Works!!
KC. How appropriate.
HENRY. What?
KC. After what you did to my generator.
BO. I'm sure it can be fixed.
HENRY. Here, KC, take my property.
KC. Don't you have any money?
HENRY. Eight dollars. Take it. And take my golds. And take my houses —
KC. Henry —
HENRY. — and take mortgaged Virginia, God love her, and take fucking B and O and fucking, fucking Water Works! Take it! Take it all. And while we're at it: Take my job, too.
KC. What?
HENRY. I don't want to work for *Me* anymore.
BO. Henry, this is hardly the time —
HENRY. Why not? We're all family here. I've thought about it long and hard, KC, and today brought it all into focus. All I've been doing — playing games. That's all it is.
KC. It's a good game. It's the best game in town. And it takes skill.
HENRY. It takes bravado, KC. It takes buzz and glitz and intimidation and style — oh God, above all: style. Well, style is nothing, KC. Not at the end of the day.
KC. Excuse me, Henry, but I will decide when you quit.
HENRY. What?

KC. I promoted you, and I will let you go. No one's leaving this ship without my say-so. It would kill us on the street.
HENRY. Sometimes I really do think you've lost all touch with reality.
KC. You know how organizations fold? Word starts leaking that there's "trouble." "Dissatisfaction with management." "Trouble in the main office." Then the vultures start circling and looking for prey. *Gourmet* will start knocking on Erna's door, or maybe the *Times*.
ERNA. Oh, do you think so?!
KC. See what I mean? No, Henry. We had a deal; you said you'd stick with me till we were Number One.
HENRY. What the hell is that, Number One?
KC. I'll know when we're it.
HENRY. But you're planning to fire me anyway, right?
BO. Oh shit … *(Pause. Rose wakes up.)*
HENRY. Admit it.
KC. So what? *(KC starts clearing tea things onto a tray.)*
HENRY. "So what"?!
KC. My firing you is one thing … and I wasn't going to "fire" you; I was going to let you go. But not if you want to. It's got to be my call. Is that perfectly clear? Bo, you sonofabitch, this must be your doing.
HENRY. No it's not; it's my doing. And you can't stop me.
KC. I can make it fiendishly difficult for you to land another job, Henry.
HENRY. In the print trade? Who wants it.
ROSE. Don't give up your job, Henry. *(They all look at her.)*
HENRY. Rose! *(He goes to her.)* Rose, honey, I have to. She's going to fire me anyway.
ROSE. Will you lose all your money?
HENRY. No, no.
KC. She's got a point, Henry. You're used to living in a style to which you were never accustomed.
HENRY. And it's led me straight into therapy.
ERNA. Winifred says —
KC. Give me your teacup, Henry. I'm going to clear these things, and then we'll have cocktails and dinner and finish the game.

HENRY.   I've already finished the game, and I think we'd all rather —

KC.   GIVE ME THE DAMN TEACUP! *(The teacup flies out of Henry's hands. Erna, in a stunning maneuver, catches it in mid-air.)*

ERNA.   Here you are, KC. May I, er …

KC.   No. *(She exits into kitchen with tea things.)*

BO.   *(Rising.)* Bravo, Henry. That was a master stroke.

ERNA.   Hear hear.

HENRY.   What?

ROSE.   Way cool, Henry.

BO.   She played right into your hand. You got your job back. Brinksmanship. I was never any good at that.

HENRY.   *(Rising.)* But I don't want my job back.

ERNA *(Rising.)* Henry, be reasonable. And think of others. If you go, I'll go. You hired me.

ROSE.   Henry, I got this friend Dwayne? He was a telemarketer. Sold home refinancing packages. He got downsized. Now he lives on a landing dock at United Parcel, unless they catch him, and then he goes to this place he knows by the old New York, New Haven and Hartford rail yards. He's homeless. And it happened … *(Snaps fingers.)* … just like that. It happens every day. *(KC returns.)*

KC.   … and should this be merely a ploy on your part, Henry, I shall of course give you the sack immediately, loudly and publicly. Got it? *(She sits.)* Now, it's my turn, and I am putting a hotel on Marvin Gardens. There's my money … Here's my lovely hotel. Bo, make drinks. *(Pause.)* Bo?

BO.   No. *(Pause.)*

KC.   What?

BO.   *(Wavering.)* I … I don't feel like a drink … Erna?

ERNA.   Well, I … No. Not really.

KC.   Henry?

HENRY.   Thanks, no.

KC.   Well, well, well. I guess I'll be drinking all by my lonesome.

ROSE.   I'd love a drink.

KC.   Oh Rose, I am sorry. I keep forgetting you. Bo?

ROSE.   Hey, no sweat. I'll get my own. *(She goes to the bar.)*

KC.   *(To Rose.)* And you can make me a … Oh, never mind. Well, why are you all standing around like little lost children?

BO. We ... we don't want to play ... Monopoly ... anymore. *(Long pause.)*
KC. Well, if you want to throw in the towel, Bo, that's neither here nor there; you'll soon be out anyway. It's really just Erna and I now. Isn't it, Erna?
ERNA. Oh ... er ... yes, I suppose so. I don't ... I don't really know what I'm doing. I really haven't the faintest notion.
KC. Henry, you have ruined a perfectly lovely afternoon. You sabotage the generator, you break up the game, you threaten me ... you are a terrorist, Henry.
BO. KC ...
KC. But terrorists don't frighten me. There's only one way to deal with them. Ignore. Ignore their petulant, selfish tactics. Which I intend to do. I shall now get dinner. It's ready. *(She starts towards kitchen.)*
ERNA. *(Softly.)* I hate eggplant. *(KC freezes in her steps.)*
KC. I beg your pardon?
ERNA. I hate eggplant. There; I said it! I loathe, despise and detest that gray, fibrous, gelatinous mess. Do you know how hard this is for a food critic to admit? I mean there's eggplant everywhere! It's all the rage: Italian, nouvelle, veggie ... there are even eggplant hoagies! And I can't go anywhere near Greece. And then there's that southern French meltdown: ratatouille, which tastes like it sounds and sounds like it looks! And it's all eggplant, eggplant, eggplant, and you're all being awful and the whole day has been awful except for one magic moment in the pump house —
KC. Bo!
ERNA. — and I just want out, can't you see, can't you help me? I just want out of this room and this eggplant and the fact that today is my fortieth birthday!! *(She collapses.)*
ROSE. Wow! Who knew? *(Sings.)* "Happy Birthday to — " *(Henry stops her. Bo takes the cellular phone out of his pocket and punches in a number, unnoticed.)*
KC. I'm not sure we need a food editor who eschews certain vegetables. I wouldn't want a music critic who disliked Brahms.
HENRY. Brahms is scarcely eggplant.
BO. Damn. No answer. *(To others:)* Armand.
KC. Armand will be out having his little drinkie. Well, I'm going

... I'm not sure where I'm going. *(She exits into kitchen.)*
ROSE. Isn't this wild?
ERNA. ... horn ...
BO. I beg your pardon?
ERNA. There was something about a horn. One blows it in case of emergency.
BO. You're right! In the closet. *(Erna dashes to the closet.)*
ERNA. Eureka! *(She holds up bullhorn.)* How does it ... *(She pushes button. Huge blast. They all fall about. KC comes running into the room.)*
KC. Who did that?! Erna! Put that down!! *(Erna is holding the horn like a gun, pointed at KC.)*
ERNA. I'm getting off of this island, do you hear? And no one's going to stop me. Not you, KC; not anyone!
KC. Give me that ... *(She starts towards Erna. Erna gives her a blast.)*
ROSE. Stop it! Stop it!!
KC. *(To Rose.)* Shut up.
ROSE. Don't you tell me to shut up!
KC. Bo ... *(Pointing to Erna.)* ... disarm that woman.
BO. I most certainly will not. Three blasts is the accepted signal, I believe. And whatever craft is nearby will —
KC. You will not make a laughingstock of me in this archipelago!
HENRY. We just want off the fucking island, KC.
KC. Wait for Armand.
HENRY. Look, KC, we've had it with Monopoly, we don't want moussaka, and we're not going to wait for Armand or Godot or anyone else. Now get out there, Erna, and blow! *(KC dashes to Erna, grabs horn. They fight. Rose comes between them, wrests horn away and runs outdoors. Erna has fallen to the floor. Three blasts are heard.)* Like the sound of Gabriel!
BO. *(Helping her up.)* Here, Erna ...
ERNA. Where's my coat ... get my coat ... *(KC stands inert in the center of the room as Bo, Erna and Henry bolt for the coat closet. Coats, scarves and rubbers are flying in all directions as they each get their outerwear. Rose comes in.)*
ROSE. I see a boat coming. Looks like a big one!
BO. Probably the Coast Guard. They're always on patrol when there's weather.

KC. It's so humiliating … We never call for help! *(She sits.)*
ERNA. Are these your things, Rose?
ROSE. Oh. Someone must've hung 'em up. *(To KC.)* Thanks.
HENRY. Here Rose … let me. *(He holds coat for her to put on.)*
ROSE. Thanks. You guys wanna come over to my place for dinner?
ERNA. I just want to get back to Manhattan!
BO. I'll drive you there.
ERNA. Thank God.
HENRY. *(To Rose.)* I'd love to come to your place, Rose.
ROSE. Don't get any funny ideas.
KC. Henry hasn't had a funny idea in months. *(Stands.)* That's why I'm replacing him!
HENRY. Good!
ROSE. Get a good severance package, Henry.
HENRY. I will, I will.
ROSE. 'Cause, you know, without money you're of no interest to me at all. *(Boat whistle heard outside.)*
BO. *(Leans out doorway.)* Ahoy! … *(Back inside:)* Go along, everyone. They've pulled up to the landing.
ERNA. Goodbye, KC … This is a birthday I shall not soon forget. *(Starts to leave, turns back:)* But the tuna melt was divine. *(She exits.)*
HENRY. Goodbye, KC. My lawyer will call yours.
KC. We've got the same lawyer.
HENRY. Well, it'll be a cheap call. *(Exit.)*
ROSE. Thanks, KC. I love all your stuff.
KC. Leave. *(Rose leaves.)*
BO. I think … I think you've gone too far, KC. You can't just run everything, you know.
KC. Why not?
BO. "I just want to run everything and always be right." That's what you said.
KC. And I do and I am. *(Pause.)*
BO. You're right, KC. You're absolutely right. *(Outside: horn.)* I hope you get your power restored. And KC?
KC. Hm?
BO. There were some lovely times. From now on, it's all business, don't you think?
KC. I'll decide that.

BO. Of course you will, KC. Of course you will. *(He exits, closes front door. Sound of launch pulling away. KC looks around, picks up an old galosh and throws it in the closet, slams closet door. She walks to the Monopoly table. Looks at board. To herself:)*

KC. If it were Erna's turn … *(She picks up dice.)* Woodjie, woodjie, woodjie … *(Throws dice.)* Nine … nine! One-two-three-four-five-six-seven-eight-nine! *(She goes to her phone and dials, waits.)* Bo? … Bo, are you on the boat? … Can you hear me? … Put Erna on! … PUT ERNA ON, GODDAMMIT! … Erna? … I just took your turn for you. I "woodjie woodjied" and rolled the dice. You were on Free Parking, Erna. The dice rolled a five and a four. That's nine, Erna, nine: Marvin Gardens, Erna. My Marvin Gardens … with a big red hotel! You owe me thousands of dollars. I win, Erna. I win. I WIN! I — *(Erna has switched off. KC sits and looks at the game board, beaming. The electric lights come on. KC looks around approvingly. Then, softly:)* I win.

End of Play

PROPERTY LIST

Money (KC)
Large grocery bag (HENRY)
Large handbag (ERNA) containing: pillow, spectacles on chain,
    airline socks, green eyeshade
Tray with two mugs, glass of water (KC)
mug of coffee (KC)
notebook, pen (ERNA)
Bloody Mary (BO)
Plate with tuna melt (KC)
Plate with hot dogs, bottle of white wine, 4 wine glasses (KC)
Glass of scotch (BO)
Matches or lighter, oil lamps (BO)
Slicker, hat (BO)
Small can cranberry juice (KC)
Cell phone (BO)
Kitchen knife (KC)
Tea pot, tray, cups, cream, sugar (KC)
Bullhorn (ERNA)

SOUND EFFECTS

Crash
Huge gust of wind
Violent thunder
Bullhorn blasts
Boat whistle
Launch pulling away

NEW PLAYS

★ **CLOSER by Patrick Marber.** Winner of the 1998 Olivier Award for Best Play and the 1999 New York Drama Critics Circle Award for Best Foreign Play. Four lives intertwine over the course of four and a half years in this densely plotted, stinging look at modern love and betrayal. "CLOSER is a sad, savvy, often funny play that casts a steely, unblinking gaze at the world of relationships and lets you come to your own conclusions ... CLOSER does not merely hold your attention; it burrows into you." –*New York Magazine* "A powerful, darkly funny play about the cosmic collision between the sun of love and the comet of desire." –*Newsweek Magazine* [2M, 2W] ISBN: 0-8222-1722-8

★ **THE MOST FABULOUS STORY EVER TOLD by Paul Rudnick.** A stage manager, headset and prompt book at hand, brings the house lights to half, then dark, and cues the creation of the world. Throughout the play, she's in control of everything. In other words, she's either God, or she thinks she is. "Line by line, Mr. Rudnick may be the funniest writer for the stage in the United States today ... One-liners, epigrams, withering put-downs and flashing repartee: These are the candles that Mr. Rudnick lights instead of cursing the darkness ... a testament to the virtues of laughing ... and in laughter, there is something like the memory of Eden." –*The NY Times* "Funny it is ... consistently, rapaciously, deliriously ... easily the funniest play in town." –*Variety* [4M, 5W] ISBN: 0-8222-1720-1

★ **A DOLL'S HOUSE by Henrik Ibsen, adapted by Frank McGuinness.** Winner of the 1997 Tony Award for Best Revival. "New, raw, gut-twisting and gripping. Easily the hottest drama this season." –*USA Today* "Bold, brilliant and alive." –*The Wall Street Journal* "A thunderclap of an evening that takes your breath away." –*Time Magazine* [4M, 4W, 2 boys] ISBN: 0-8222-1636-1

★ **THE HERBAL BED by Peter Whelan.** The play is based on actual events which occurred in Stratford-upon-Avon in the summer of 1613, when William Shakespeare's elder daughter was publicly accused of having a sexual liaison with a married neighbor and family friend. "In his probing new play, THE HERBAL BED ... Peter Whelan muses about a sidelong event in the life of Shakespeare's family and creates a finely textured tapestry of love and lies in the early 17th-century Stratford." –*The NY Times* "It is a first rate drama with interesting moral issues of truth and expediency." –*The NY Post* [5M, 3W] ISBN: 0-8222-1675-2

★ **SNAKEBIT by David Marshall Grant.** A study of modern friendship when put to the test. "... a rather smart and absorbing evening of water-cooler theater, the intimate sort of Off-Broadway experience that has you picking apart the recognizable characters long after the curtain calls." –*The NY Times* "Off-Broadway keeps on presenting us with compelling reasons for going to the theater. The latest is SNAKEBIT, David Marshall Grant's smart new comic drama about being thirtysomething and losing one's way in life." –*The NY Daily News* [3M, 1W] ISBN: 0-8222-1724-4

★ **A QUESTION OF MERCY by David Rabe.** The Obie Award-winning playwright probes the sensitive and controversial issue of doctor-assisted suicide in the age of AIDS in this poignant drama. "There are many devastating ironies in Mr. Rabe's beautifully considered, piercingly clear-eyed work ..." –*The NY Times* "With unsettling candor and disturbing insight, the play arouses pity and understanding of a troubling subject ... Rabe's provocative tale is an affirmation of dignity that rings clear and true." –*Variety* [6M, 1W] ISBN: 0-8222-1643-4

★ **DIMLY PERCEIVED THREATS TO THE SYSTEM by Jon Klein.** Reality and fantasy overlap with hilarious results as this unforgettable family attempts to survive the nineties. "Here's a play whose point about fractured families goes to the heart, mind – and ears." –*The Washington Post* "... an end-of-the millennium comedy about a family on the verge of a nervous breakdown ... Trenchant and hilarious ..." –*The Baltimore Sun* [2M, 4W] ISBN: 0-8222-1677-9

DRAMATISTS PLAY SERVICE, INC.
440 Park Avenue South, New York, NY 10016 212-683-8960 Fax 212-213-1539
postmaster@dramatists.com www.dramatists.com

NEW PLAYS

★ **AS BEES IN HONEY DROWN by Douglas Carter Beane.** Winner of the John Gassner Playwriting Award. A hot young novelist finds the subject of his new screenplay in a New York socialite who leads him into the world of *Auntie Mame* and *Breakfast at Tiffany's*, before she takes him for a ride. "A delicious soufflé of a satire … [an] extremely entertaining fable for an age that always chooses image over substance." *–The NY Times* "… A witty assessment of one of the most active and relentless industries in a consumer society … the creation of 'hot' young things, which the media have learned to mass produce with efficiency and zeal." *–The NY Daily News* [3M, 3W, flexible casting] ISBN: 0-8222-1651-5

★ **STUPID KIDS by John C. Russell.** In rapid, highly stylized scenes, the story follows four high-school students as they make their way from first through eighth period and beyond, struggling with the fears, frustrations, and longings peculiar to youth. "In STUPID KIDS … playwright John C. Russell gets the opera of adolescence to a T … The stylized teenspeak of STUPID KIDS … suggests that Mr. Russell may have hidden a tape recorder under a desk in study hall somewhere and then scoured the tapes for good quotations … it is the kids' insular, ceaselessly churning world, a pre-adult world of Doritos and libidos, that the playwright seeks to lay bare." *–The NY Times* "STUPID KIDS [is] a sharp-edged … whoosh of teen angst and conformity anguish. It is also very funny." *–NY Newsday* [2M, 2W] ISBN: 0-8222-1698-1

★ **COLLECTED STORIES by Donald Margulies.** From Obie Award-winner Donald Margulies comes a provocative analysis of a student-teacher relationship that turns sour when the protégé becomes a rival. "With his fine ear for detail, Margulies creates an authentic, insular world, and he gives equal weight to the opposing viewpoints of two formidable characters." *–The LA Times* "This is probably Margulies' best play to date …" *–The NY Post* "… always fluid and lively, the play is thick with ideas, like a stock-pot of good stew." *–The Village Voice* [2W] ISBN: 0-8222-1640-X

★ **FREEDOMLAND by Amy Freed.** An overdue showdown between a son and his father sets off fireworks that illuminate the neurosis, rage and anxiety of one family – and of America at the turn of the millennium. "FREEDOMLAND's more obvious links are to *Buried Child* and *Bosoms and Neglect*. Freed, like Guare, is an inspired wordsmith with a gift for surreal touches in situations grounded in familiar and real territory." *–Curtain Up* [3M, 4W] ISBN: 0-8222-1719-8

★ **STOP KISS by Diana Son.** A poignant and funny play about the ways, both sudden and slow, that lives can change irrevocably. "There's so much that is vital and exciting about STOP KISS … you want to embrace this young author and cheer her onto other works … the writing on display here is funny and credible … you also will be charmed by its heartfelt characters and up-to-the-minute humor." *–The NY Daily News* "… irresistibly exciting … a sweet, sad, and enchantingly sincere play." *–The NY Times* [3M, 3W] ISBN: 0-8222-1731-7

★ **THREE DAYS OF RAIN by Richard Greenberg.** The sins of fathers and mothers make for a bittersweet elegy in this poignant and revealing drama. "… a work so perfectly judged it heralds the arrival of a major playwright … Greenberg is extraordinary." *–The NY Daily News* "Greenberg's play is filled with graceful passages that are by turns melancholy, harrowing, and often, quite funny." *–Variety* [2M, 1W] ISBN: 0-8222-1676-0

★ **THE WEIR by Conor McPherson.** In a bar in rural Ireland, the local men swap spooky stories in an attempt to impress a young woman from Dublin who recently moved into a nearby "haunted" house. However, the tables are soon turned when she spins a yarn of her own. "You shed all sense of time at this beautiful and devious new play." *–The NY Times* "Sheer theatrical magic. I have rarely been so convinced that I have just seen a modern classic. Tremendous." *–The London Daily Telegraph* [4M, 1W] ISBN: 0-8222-1706-6

DRAMATISTS PLAY SERVICE, INC.
440 Park Avenue South, New York, NY 10016 212-683-8960 Fax 212-213-1539
postmaster@dramatists.com   www.dramatists.com